The Long Shot

*Rebirth of a
Forgotten Riverfront*

DIDmedia
PUBLICATIONS

The Long Shot

Rebirth of a Forgotten Riverfront

MY STORY BY

MARK BENNETT

Thanks to God

for the awesome beauty

of His creation and the

privilege we've been given

to be a part of it.

DEDICATION

He singlehandedly changed the face of the North Augusta Riverfront.

Through his vision, determination, and perseverance he managed to achieve what so many said could never happen. So, when he told me he was writing a book detailing the creation of the River Club, I could not have been happier.

It's important for the people of North Augusta to learn the true story of how the South Carolina side of the Savannah River came to be what it is today—but this story is a life lesson for anyone who's faced insurmountable odds in trying to reach a goal.

Although my father's name is nowhere to be seen, my family and I know the cost he truly paid to see his dream become a beautiful reality. The game of golf means so much to this family because, over the years as we've spent countless hours on the golf course together, he's taught me so many things about the game and, more importantly, about life.

This book will give you a glimpse into the kind of quality man he is. We love him, we are proud of him, and we are striving to be more like him every day.

—JASON BENNETT

MARK BENNETT

INTRODUCTION

He hitched up his knickers, checked the prevailing breeze, paused and then gazed at his target, a 4 ½ inch cup some 235 yards away. He could see the sun's glare shimmering on the pond that stretched across the front of the 15th green. He hesitated for just a moment, checking his yardage for the final and last time and casually asked his caddie for a four wood. It was said that he swung so hard that he lost his balance but stood there watching as the ball flew into golf history.

Golf fans know that as "the shot heard around the world." It was the final round of the second-ever Masters Tournament and the only double eagle (albatross) ever recorded at the 15th hole during Masters play. That long shot was played April 7, 1935, hit by a short, stocky ball striker by the name of Gene Sarazen. He hit a 2 on a par 5 which tied him for the lead with Craig Wood, who lost their 36-hole playoff the following day by 5 strokes.

In all honesty, I don't know a lot more about Gene Sarazen's other heroics in his golfing career other than he was the first player to win "golf's career grand slam." What I do know about Gene Sarazen is that he had the guts to play the shot. That decision he made while standing there in the middle of the 15th fairway changed his life forever and in the process added some mystique that still surrounds the 15th hole as players today still try to equal that long shot. That's the good stuff, the things that keep us playing the game, the opportunity to meet the challenge and win.

Just suppose for a moment, what if a strong gust of wind, lurking behind those tall pines on the 16th hole, started swirling once the ball was in flight? A two turns into a six or even worse, and a historic golf moment is deleted from the pages of golf lore. Until that moment, Mr. Sarazen had done everything right; was focused, resolved, and hit the ball solidly, but the results were disastrous. Through no fault of his own, the outcome changed everything. I can almost hear golf analysts saying, "That's golf —the golf gods were not smiling today."

There are a lot of similarities in playing the long shot, both on the golf course and in life—we all take them. On the golf course, the hurt, the defeat, the highs and lows. It all stops there... or at least it usually does, by the time we tee it up again. In life, it is not so easy. Some of the long shots in life take a lifetime to recover, if we ever do.

The story that follows is one of those long shots. I call it the longest of long shots because everyone was telling me it couldn't be done, since there was no financial safety net to catch me if I failed. What they didn't know is that I knew I could do it.

The challenge of turning a worthless piece of real estate into a championship golf course—267 acres located just 3 miles from the Augusta National Golf Club—was my vision. This land would become the canvas on which I would mold and shape a unique championship golf course out of a forgotten riverfront.

Making it happen was my long shot.

THE LAND
AND THE LEGEND

Determining a story's origin, where it really begins, can be a most difficult task. And it's true in this story because it revolves around a unique piece of God's creation, a piece of terra-firma, a measure of dirt worth very little as it lies relative to the rest of the world. At least that's the way I imagine it was in the beginning. But God in His infinite wisdom knew if His master plan was going to be realized, this particular 330-acre tract of land would have to be situated south of the Mason-Dixon Line, somewhere in the deep South along the banks of a mighty river, a river that would eventually play a major role in the development of the land and the future events that took place there. The land He selected would be located inland, exactly 202 river miles from His newly-created Atlantic Ocean. This river would later become known as the Savannah, separating the land into two of the original 13 colonies. The one to the north would be called South Carolina, and the colony to the south, named after King George III, called Georgia.

Only God knows how long that river flowed to the ocean before men actually tried to go up it. But it's a known fact that prior to our ancestors arriving, the red man treated the fertile soil along the Savannah as sacred ground. So much so, that the tribes of Yuchi, Yemassee and Chippewa battled and massacred each other trying to possess it. From its tranquil beginning, this much sought-after piece of ground was drenched and stained with blood and over time tried by fire. As Spanish and French explorers continued this mayhem, they discovered the mouth of the Savannah and forged inland, opening the way for others to follow. In 1650, one of these explorers, an Englishman named Oglethorpe, founded a settlement on the Georgia side of the river and called it Augusta. That name stuck. It's a name known around the world, not so much for its founder, but for its golf and one of the game's greatest players, the legendary Bobby Jones.

At the risk of getting ahead of my story, let me interject since so much of this tale has to do with my passion for the game of golf. As a teenager growing up in Augusta, local high school golf teams would man the scoreboards at the Augusta National Golf Club. I worked the 16th hole scoreboard, hanging on a ladder with one arm around it, flipping mostly green numbers (and occasionally a red one) with the other hand. We were given our assignments and instructions a week prior to the tournament. Mr. Jones, although confined to a wheelchair, would conduct those meetings which were usually held right outside the pro shop annex. He wheeled himself to the highest point to be visible, then made sure each one of us understood how important our job was and that we should be careful to treat patrons as special guests. Afterward, he took the time to shake each of our hands and catch our names.

No doubt, I was privileged to personally meet the man

who ushered in the modern era of golf. He made a tremendous impact on the game and on me. There are volumes of books written about Bobby Jones and his triumphant Grand Slam as an amateur. As gifted a player as he was, what I found even more impressive about Mr. Jones was his dignity and character. His ability to "play it as it lays," both on the golf course and in life, was proven.

He believed that when you play the ball down, never touching it, the results after the ball is played are meant to be, whether good or bad. If you improve your lie, the results have been fabricated and should consequently reduce the total number of strokes taken on the hole.

But then you are left with the nagging question, "Were the results a product of my talent, or is my ability limited to just playing the easy shots and ignoring the rules?" I've found that life is seldom easy, and as hard we may try, no one gets through life unscathed.

This story, with all its twists and turns, chronicles my quest to follow a dream that seized my imagination and held me in its grasp until it nearly suffocated me.

In the process, I discovered the limits of talent and the gut-wrenching price one has to pay to make a vision come true.

HENRY SCHULTZ: FROM DREAM TO DECEPTION

In the same year our country was declaring its independence from Britain, on the other side of the world in a quiet German village a young mother was giving birth to her son. She named him Henry. As with all of us, some choices God doesn't give us. The exact time, place and pedigree of our bloodline are solely within His providence. So it was with Henry. Even though he was born in poverty, Henry was determined to elevate himself out of this hostile environment. But subsequent events of time and fate would ultimately have a greater impact on his life and future than anything he could ever imagine.

At that time all of Europe was engulfed in the Napoleonic War, and the historical account of young Henry's life documents his contempt for the invading French army. In defense of his family and homeland, he took up arms against the Germans and was taken captive shortly after fighting broke out near Hamburg, Germany. He escaped, was later recaptured and sentenced to death. His mother, upon hearing the verdict, pleaded with the court to spare her son's life. The judge, knowing Henry's young age, and with the threat of more violence from the townspeople, agreed to suspend the death sentence and ordered Henry to be exiled to America immediately.

Fate had dealt Henry a cruel blow, or so it would seem if our story ended there. Historical records offer no details of the events that took place between his forced departure from Hamburg to his mysterious arrival to this country. Being a German immigrant in a foreign country, unfamiliar with the language, penniless and alone, Henry made a significant contribution to the economic growth of the South through sheer determination and an unyielding spirit. Specifically, it was Henry's fascination with acquiring a promising tract of land, subduing it and making it his. That's how the legend was born: The Legend of Henry Schultz.

Legend only: that's how I first came to know Henry some 170 years later. We shared a deep passion and respect for the same piece of ground that is situated directly across the river from Augusta's bustling commercial district. It is irreverent to call it just an ordinary piece of ground, in light of what it has had to endure over the last two centuries. What Henry must have seen when he first gazed at this virgin landscape was land endowed with towering pine trees, magnificent live oaks, maples and sycamores gracefully touching the water's edge. Interspersed among these trees were dogwoods, redbuds and native azaleas reflecting an array of spring colors shimmering against the cool waters of the Savannah.

His emotions must have been similar to those of golfers Bobby Jones and Cliff Roberts as they experienced the drive up Magnolia Lane for first time. Of course, it wasn't Magnolia Lane then. It was just a red Georgia clay driveway lined on both sides with newly-planted southern magnolias.

These visionary men saw and recognized immediately the immense beauty and promising potential Fruitland Nurseries held for creating America's finest inland golf course—the Augusta National Golf Club. It's hard to imagine which one of these gentlemen first said it, but I'd like to think it was Bobby who said, "This is it! We found it!" The decision was made and their work began.

That same exhilarating feeling surely overtook Henry some hundred and twenty years earlier when he first laid eyes on a 330-acre site on the South Carolina side of the Savannah River, directly across from the heart of Augusta, and realized his life's work. It's hard to know exactly what motivated him, besides the obvious ones that drive most entrepreneurs. Was it simply the opportunity to make money? No, I believe it was more than that. He saw and felt the pulse of his era. He was driven by the same desire that drives all men of vision: a passionate need to create, to improve society and maybe transform the world in some small way. And for a time, he did transform this wild stretch of river from an alligator-infested swamp into a proper town he named Hamburg.

One evening in the fall of 1992, I came to know Henry in a very personal way. I had often heard the local tales about Henry Schultz and the unfortunate demise of both his prosperity and his great dream. But the dusty pages of history were about to spring open in apparent reality for me.

I found myself walking the site of old Hamburg with our golf course contractor who had begun clearing and grubbing the center lines of the fairways. Some areas of the site were so densely covered with undergrowth that it was impossible to see where you were walking. Jerry, the dozer operator, carefully maneuvered between trees, making a path for us to follow. Everything was working

Artist rendering of Schultz, from a verbal description of the man.

fine. We were beginning to see progress when all of a sudden the left track of the dozer collapsed into in a hole. That is not too uncommon as sometimes tree stumps will decay below the ground and with time become covered with litter. In this particular instance, however, we immediately knew that wasn't the case. We could tell by the sound of falling dirt and the way Jerry almost fell from the cab that we had hit a deep hole. With the right track still on solid ground, Jerry was able to back the heavy piece of equipment out, revealing an eerie piece of North Augusta's history.

There he was, unearthed and exposed in broad daylight for the whole damn world to see. It never occurred to us that one of these shallow depressions could be a gravesite. What was once just a myth and only a legend was no longer just a myth. It had to be Henry—his final wish was to be buried standing up, with his back to Augusta, as a final expression of disgust for those who conspired to ruin him. A cold piece of granite which served as a mighty poor excuse for a tombstone hung over the edge of the hole.

It looked as though his headstone must have fallen over face down, preserving its inscription in mint condition. Considering all of his accomplishments, you would think his epitaph would have been engraved with some inspiring words cerebrating his life. Instead the words, 'Here Lies Henry Schultz 1776-1851. In Death I Stand, Never Having Looked Up to Any Man.'

Jerry, in his classic South Georgia drawl, muttered,

"What the hellah we done done?"

I don't believe in ghosts, spirits or Ouija boards, and certainly I don't believe that old Henry, crazy as he was, would take his vengeance out on me for disturbing his place of solitude. Out of decency or the fear of violating some federal law, we fixed Henry's exact location by measuring distances between some specimen mulberry trees that were slated to remain undisturbed. Jerry quickly climbed back up in the cab of the dozer, fired her up, made a few passes over Henry, and the scene faded to black in my mind.

At that moment, I awoke in a cold sweat, slowly realizing that this graphic encounter wasn't real at all—but a figment of my subconscious. Nightmares like this one were to reappear without warning many times over the next few years, as my love of golf and my own vision to resurrect Henry's ghostly village moved from the shadows into stark reality. I can only assume that Henry must have left an indelible curse on this piece of land—which was surely his deathbed response to a life fighting the human greed that ultimately killed his dream. I would realize much too late that his life experience and mine had merged onto parallel tracks, proving the old adage that 'if we fail to learn the lessons of history, we are doomed to repeat them.'

Enough about myths and dreams. Here are the facts.

Henry had arrived in America in the early 1800's and made his way south, securing employment on a river barge transporting cotton and tobacco up and down the Savannah River to the ports of Charleston and Savannah. Maybe it was his love and familiarity with the river, knowing its every bend and the exact location of every navigable channel that inspired him to start dreaming, or maybe it was just day-dreaming, something to while away the time as the water splashed against this huge flat-bottom

Cotton boats laden with hundreds of bales found their way up the Savannah to the port of Augusta in the years leading up to the Civil War.

mud-scraper. Whatever, after eight long years pushing and pulling this lumbering river giant off every snag and sandbar in the river, Henry had earned and stashed away enough cash to take the necessary actions to start turning his dreams into reality. So he purchased his own barge and hired other folks to do the pushing and pulling.

Cotton was king during this era of the South's commercial development, and Augusta, Georgia was where thousands of bales were delivered every fall. Cotton made its way through Augusta on its voyage to European markets from plantations as far away as Tennessee, traveling by mule-drawn wagons over rutted clay roads and primitive trails. I'm told it wasn't uncommon to see those old wooden mule wagons in a variety of all shapes and sizes lined up five miles back in every direction clambering to get to Augusta's Cotton Exchange. Of course, it was in Georgia's best interest to make sure this valuable commodity, once loaded and on its way down river, arrived routinely and unloaded on the Savannah docks. This created a large disparity in the cotton trade between the two rivaling states which greatly favored Georgia.

Henry's early success came from his great expertise in the transportation of cotton and his skill in moving a great deal of it. While traveling in and out of these two rivaling port cities on a regular basis, Henry saw and heard what was happening and was convinced he had a plan that would tip this trade imbalance in Carolina's favor. Certainly he wasn't the only one who saw this as an opportunity. Other entrepreneurs and well-heeled businessmen had to be aware of all the latest gossip and news circulating in the port cities of Charleston and Savannah. Who knows? Maybe they even conceived the idea. But the difference was, Henry had the guts and obviously the desire and determination to pull it off. To this day, 170

PHOTO: ASHLEY BENNETT

Granite pillars bear silent witness to the ambitious entrepreneurship of Henry's Augusta Bridge.

Henry Schultz's Augusta Bridge in 1816, as shown on one of his bank's "Bridge Bills." (Courtesy of Carl Anderson and David Marsh in Georgia Obsolete Currency.)

years later, the remnants of his idea, granite pillars, still linger proudly in the surging waters of the Savannah River, right across from downtown Augusta. Building a bridge, a toll bridge—that was his brainstorm.

Most all the cotton and tobacco grown in the uplands of Carolina had to be loaded on tow barges, poled across the river and unloaded in Augusta. Once these precious handpicked commodities crossed the river, there was no way they were going to end up on Charleston's docks, thus the great state of South Carolina would continue losing its battle to collect its fair share of taxes. To this day, rivalry still exists between these two southeastern port cities.

Building a covered wooden bridge to span the river, some 250 yards, was no small endeavor, not to mention coming up with the funds to pay for its construction. There was also the challenge of getting legislative approvals to cross the river from both states. Even in those early days, government involvement was prerequisite. In Henry's quest to secure funding for his ambitious project, he opened the Bridge Bank and issued $600,000 in bank notes that would be secured and redeemed by future toll revenues. At the age of thirty-three, Henry sold the bridge to his business partner, John McKinne, who assumed all financial obligations to pay off the outstanding balance on the note that amounted to a little over $12,000 due to the State of Georgia Bank. McKinne, who was also a board member of the bank, defaulted on the note and surrendered the bridge to the bank. In other words, the bank bought the bridge for a mere $12,000, an asset that was generating annual revenues in excess of that amount.

I imagine it was all legal. Henry's problem was he trusted his partner and failed to read the fine print. For years Henry tried in vain to seek a legal remedy to pay off the note and regain procession of the bridge. It never happened. It had to be disheartening that all of his efforts and perseverance had come to this. His entrepreneurial spirit that was once driven by his dreams and visions of making a significant contribution to mankind had encountered something he had never contemplated: greed. From that day forth, Henry's motivations changed from doing good to getting even. Henry was outraged and vowed vengeance against those who had plotted against him, the bank, its board members and the City of Augusta.

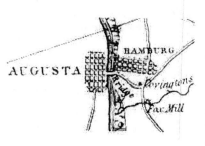

You certainly can't blame Henry, but the cost of exacting vengeance comes at great peril to those seeking restitution. What good is it, if at the end of the day you become that which you are seeking to destroy? Legend has it that Henry lost all confidence in his fellow man. He became a recluse, his bitterness growing with each passing day.

Out of his hatred for Augusta, he focused all his attention on the 270 acres on the South Carolina side of the river and concentrated his efforts on building a new town that he hoped would eventually eclipse Augusta as the

The Augusta Bridge, pictured as it appeared in 1850, with Hamburg visible across the river and the Augusta Wharf in the foreground.

Hamburg in 1872, by C. N. Drie, courtesy of the Augusta History Museum. The sturdy, elegant Augusta Bridge is visible at upper left, and served the public until 1888, when it was severely damaged in a flood. It was virtually abandoned leading up to the Civil War, but repopulated afterward as a settlement for former slaves. The town was finally obliterated in 1929 as a massive double flood swept down the Savannah.

center of commerce. It's amazing what hatred can accomplish. Hatred was the foundation on which Henry built his town. He named it Hamburg after his German hometown.

In a manner worthy of a modern-day city planner, Henry had strategically laid out his master plan to take full advantage of the toll bridge that was now in the hands of his competitors. Within just two years, Augusta was beginning to take notice of Henry's threats to get even. First, Henry cleared the land along the river's edge, then constructed a two hundred foot long wharf complete with several warehouses and a dock to accommodate a profitable steamboat line running between Hamburg and Charleston. At the interior of the site a variety of shops were all neatly clustered and planned around a large bowling green common area. Also included were a large mercantile center, a doctor's office, and a printing press. Homes were integrated as well. It's easy to imagine how vibrant Hamburg must have been in the evenings with sounds of river traffic, jangle of buggies, dogs barking and the subtle glow of street lamps casting faint light in the river.

Henry's Hamburg was the same piece of land my partner and I discovered back in the mid-seventies while working with a group that included Mayor Pop Newman, Jim Cullum and several other community leaders. Together, we explored how Augusta's riverfront might best be developed as a means of encouraging retail businesses to stay loyal to downtown Augusta and not be lured away by the malls. This brainstorming exercise planted the seed in my imagination that would ultimately express itself as a full-blown riverfront concept based on my great love of golf.

As my personal interest in this property began to grow, my attorney Zack Everett, who had the daunting task of clearing title for our insurance provider, also made me

The land between the Fifth Street and Thirteenth Street Bridges in its natural state: a wilderness home for egrets and waterfowl of all kinds, as well as numerous alligators and snakes.

aware of Hamburg's history and the huge problems associated with existing road right-of-ways that clouded title to the property. It seemed they were indelibly etched on the land and fighting it out in court to legally resolve the matter. Over the years, the original 270 acres of land had been busted-up, parceled off, and subdivided many times, reflecting only a vague resemblance of Henry's model town. After years of neglect, abuse, and exploitation only one family remained out of the original seventy that resided on the property in 1823. And they lived in a green painted concrete block house, right-smack-dab in the middle of hole number one of the beautiful new golf course I had now begun to envision on that site.

Like my partner John Thomas and me, Henry was a visionary, an entrepreneur, and a risk-taker. He left his footprints all over the property. Now it would become our turn to pick up the pieces that remained of Hamburg, certainly not with vengeance, but with a shared passion to create.

My father, mother and me at the restaurant

SON OF THE SOUTH

My personal story begins in the deep South. Charleston, South Carolina is where I was born on September 1, 1945. My mom, from my earliest recollection, made me aware this was the same day General MacArthur signed the peace treaty with Japan. For some strange reason, mom seemed to get a great deal of satisfaction from calling me her "peace-time baby."

I have no memory of those early days in Charleston except those recalled by my older sisters, who were saddled with the responsibility of rearing this snotty-nosed, skinny kid. Connie was the oldest; next were Gail and Harriett, followed by me and my brother Richard, who inherited the proud title "Mama's Baby Boy."

As a kid and later as a man, I watched my sisters turn into some of the most attractive women I would ever have the privilege to know. Not only were they good looking — they were smart as well, which eventually led to a great deal of difficulty explaining to my dad why my grades couldn't compare to theirs. My dad's motto was, "You can never have enough education." Somewhere around the third grade, I knew we were not in agreement on this point.

I'm told we moved to Augusta, Georgia in the late

1940s to be close to my grandparents. Mom's parents had a modest amount of land on Milledgeville Road and gave Mom and Dad a couple acres there to get started in their new restaurant business. Dad's parents also lived in Augusta, on Merry Street, but they both passed away before I was old enough to remember much about them.

I don't know why it is, but as I look back, most all of my relatives—grandparents, aunts and uncles—were a dichotomy, so to speak. All the women were raised in the Protestant faith as good, God-fearing women who considered their marriage vows a sacred obligation. You know, the part that says love, honor and obey? They took that literally: divorce, for whatever reason, was unspeakable.

Dad was a complicated man. When he spoke or asked one of us kids to do something, we knew better than to ask questions — we just did it! Over the years I've tried to find some sort of justification for his behavior. All I can say is it must have been related to a medical problem that he experienced as a child that affected the physical condition of his heart in later years. As a child Dad had a bout with rheumatic fever that went untreated because his parents, unable to foot the medical bills, were too proud to ask for financial help or any other kind of help from anyone.

My father was very intelligent, well read, and was able to fix anything electrical or mechanical. He was one of nine brothers and sisters, all of whom had made a pact among themselves to improve their humble circumstances by obtaining a college education. Their plan, so I'm told, was to save a few dollars out of each week's pay in order to accumulate enough money to pay for the oldest sibling's education. Then in turn, when that individual graduated and was on his feet, the responsibility fell on him to assist in financing the next child's education.

All was going well until it was Dad's turn to go college. By this time, Dad (Herman) had met and fallen in love with my mom, a dark-haired beauty named Cora who lived out on Milledgeville Road. The chain was broken. Herman married Cora, they had five kids. Of course, some of my aunts and uncles on Dad's side blamed Cora for breaking the chain, which in turn created a well-hidden rift between the Bennetts and the Peacocks.

Mom, on the other hand, was a reflection of her mother Hattie, a dyed-in-the-wool, born-again believer. She was the definition of a hard-working, spirit-filled and loving woman. Grandma's father was a Methodist preacher, and she inherited his talent for quoting the scriptures word for word, chapter and verse. Her King James Version bold-print Bible was her prized procession with its faded, worn pages sprinkled with colored lithograph prints depicting biblical events. Grandma must have read the Bible through at least a hundred times and, for a woman with little formal education, she was blessed with a lot of common sense.

She was our family matriarch. When problems arose — and with a family as large as ours they were abundant — Grandma was always there to help ease the load with her gentle words of wisdom. Regardless of the size of the problem, she believed that everything happened for a reason... that in adversity, God is trying to tell us something or teach us some kind of lesson. Her favorite adage was, "Where there's a will, there's a way." Over the years, in times of great desperation, her strong belief came back to comfort me again and again.

Granddaddy, on the other hand, was a real piece of work. He came from a generation of hard workers, where education didn't count for much. But what he lacked in reading and writing skills he more than made up for with his degree in "raising hell." I don't think granddaddy could say more than two words at a time without an expletive spewing out of his foul mouth. Grandma and some of the rest of the family had gotten so used to his language they could tune it out. But occasionally, he would get our attention and send us all into shell-shock with some new descriptive adjective that we had never heard before. What made this so bizarre was that, in the midst of all his high-volume cussing and commotion, everyone around him would quote scripture verses, trying to prove their point of view. Apparently, their ultimate goal was to try to convince each other they had received God's Great Commission, and preaching the gospel was the only way to confront Grandpa.

While all this soul-saving was going on, the Civil Rights movement was just cranking up and my folks, like most southerners, didn't like it one damn bit. Black folk were being told to step to the rear of the bus, which was a humiliating experience for them and embarrassing for me to witness. But since most of our neighbors were black, I couldn't understand why my folks, so fervently spiritual, seemed to have such a problem with equal rights. Besides, what about the part in the Book that has to do with The Golden Rule?

Drinking alcohol wasn't permitted in my family, at least not in public. The only time I saw my parents or any of my relatives take a drink was at the communion table, and that was just a sip of Mogen David wine. But the infamous Havana Club was directly across the street from my folks' drive-in restaurant, which also happens to be the place we called home. That might sound a little strange, but to us at that time, it seemed pretty normal. Our house wasn't exactly what I would call typical, not even for the fifties. It was a workplace. Neither my sisters nor I ever felt comfortable having friends over, but what the heck, they weren't any better off than we were. Nevertheless, our neighborhood was only three miles from the "Hill Section" and the Augusta National Golf Club. But we were nestled in the northwest part of what's known as Nellieville. That was where I grew up—my "Pottersville."

Nellieville may have been my home, but it certainly wasn't where I lived. I lived somewhere in my imagination. I had inherited some drawing talent, which was enough to cause my grammar school teachers to compete with each other to get me in their class. While my classmates were learning their ABC's, I was stuck off in a corner doing bulletin boards, which included nature and landscape drawing. It gave me time to fine-tune my ability, including proper perspective in rendering objects and buildings. This early experience would greatly help prepare me for the discipline I chose in college: Landscape Architecture.

Nellieville was about one-and-a-half square miles in size, sitting on the edge of Augusta's city limits. Its population was predominantly black with a few token white families sprinkled around its perimeter. In the early fifties, its northern boundary, Milledgeville Road, was the major paved two-lane corridor running between Camp Gordon and downtown Augusta, and this busy highway fueled Mom's drive-in restaurant business. Nellieville was a hodgepodge of family-owned businesses and single-family residences filled with common folk, both black and white, who were fortunate enough to have the ingenuity to build their own shelters for their families.

All my folks were pretty good builders, and "Bennett's Drive-In Restaurant," our home sweet home, was surrounded by a variety of business establishments. On the opposite side of the road, directly in front of Mom's restaurant, was that infamous Havana Club. What a place! Our house was the only one in the neighborhood where you could stand outside and get high without ever having to take a drink, compliments of the bar across the street.

On one hot summer night, several GI's crossed the street to our house from the Havana Club after having a few too many. Things started out okay—they just wanted some of Mom's home cooking. So, as usual, one of my sisters went over to take their order and they got fresh. It quickly got out of control to the extent that Mom threatened to call the cops. Their abusive behavior and vulgar language continued throughout the course of their meal, after which they left and returned to the Havana Club.

Unfortunately, it didn't end there. When Dad got home from work, he heard what had taken place only moments earlier. Without saying a word, his face turned red as fire and he was out the door. Mom tried stopping him, but to no avail. He was going to teach those guys some Southern manners. Dad had a helluva of a temper, and we all knew that when it blew, anything could happen and usually did. Physically, Dad was a little over six feet tall and a solid one-hundred eighty pounds. There wasn't an ounce of fat on him. He was one lean, mean, fighting machine ready for revenge as he crossed the street and burst through the front doors, with fists clinched. Just as abruptly, he flew out the back door with all three GI's kicking his butt.

Uncle CB ran towards the commotion and dragged Dad back across the street to our home. Those GI's thought it was all over, but it wasn't. Dad could hardly speak, but he managed to mumble the words, "I swear I'll get those S.O.B.'s."

Although Dad was a complicated man, he was a man of few words. Everyone who knew Dad gave him plenty of room, including me. Those GI's had made a bad mistake; they just didn't know it yet. It was only after dad's death, when I was getting my own butt kicked on the Cabbage

Patch Golf Course by Uncle CB, that he revealed the end of the story. The way he recalled it, several months had passed since the "GI incident" when on a Saturday afternoon, while they were driving downtown on Broad Street in Augusta, Dad suddenly hollered, "Stop the car! Stop the car! There's one of them!" Before Uncle CB could stop the car, Dad jumped out and started beating the hell out of the guy. It was over in a matter of a couple minutes. Dad jumped back in the car and said, "One down and two to go." I don't know if he ever got the others or not, but I'll bet he never stopped looking.

Thank God, things weren't always that exciting. When Dad wasn't around, life was pretty normal; but when we saw his truck parked in the backyard, it was time to be on our best behavior. It was always "Yes Sir, No Sir, Yes Ma'am, No Ma'am." During those years, I think most Southern folks, regardless of color, practiced the same high regard for their elders. This pattern of respect served me well during my stint in the military.

Another piece of real estate that monopolized a lot of our time growing up was a vacant cornfield owned by my grandparents which had been converted into a Gospel Picture Drive-in Theater. A fire and brimstone preacher from up the street had no trouble convincing Grandma that admission must be free to the general public and that any charitable donations would help grow God's Kingdom. All the women in the family supported the idea, so instead of sitting on Grandma's front porch in the evening, they stuck all the kids in the back of Dad's Dodge pick-up truck and drove off to the movies.

The menfolk, however, didn't have much to say in spiritual matters. They just wanted to keep peace in the family, so they learned to roll their eyes and keep their mouths shut. They left the soul-saving to the women and did all they could to refrain from talking about religion in any form or fashion. Dad was in that category. He never went to church with the rest of us, so every Sunday morning Mom would get all gussied-up, put on her finest hat and drag my sisters and me out the door to church. Dad always had some lame excuse for not going with us, but that never deterred Mom from being faithful. She and my Aunt Eloise were there every time the doors opened.

It wasn't until I was about eight or nine years old that I decided if Dad didn't need to go to church, neither did I. So I told Mom I wasn't going anymore, and all hell broke loose. Guess who eventually went to church? You got it: Dad. Now he was dragging me to church instead of Mom. My ploy had backfired.

It was on a Sunday morning that an incident occurred which typifies the 1950s-era racial hatred and deplorable behavior that many southern men exhibited, including my father. I think if I hadn't been there that morning, he would have lived out the balance of his life behind bars.

My memory of it is as clear now as if it had happened yesterday. Mom's Restaurant had been converted into a full-service gas station which continued to be our home, and Sundays were "going-to-meeting" days. Mom badgered Dad not to open the filling station on the Lord's Day and, as usual, he paid her no mind.

The incident started when Dad's one black employee came to work drunk. My father fired the man on the spot, gave him his pay and told him to get off the property, whereby he responded with, "Kiss my ass. I'm not leaving." Without saying a word, Dad busted the man in the head. He hit him so hard he broke his hand, yet the man, either dazed or drunk, refused to leave. With that, my father came tearing through the house, went directly to the closet where he kept his double-barreled shotgun, grabbed a handful of shells and headed back out the front door to shoot the man. Mom, bless her heart, tried to keep him from going out the door by hanging onto his trousers, but he shook her off like a mad dog and continued out the door. Meanwhile, all the white men from surrounding businesses had jumped into the fight and by the time Dad got back with the shotgun, they had the man pinned face down on the ground.

It was sort of like a Rodney King incident without police involvement. I disobeyed my father after he told us, "Stay inside the house and don't come out," which is like asking someone not to watch a house on fire: it's impossible.

Once outside, I managed to weasel my way through the angry mob that was shouting, "Shoot him, Herman, go on and shoot him." In disbelief I watched my father load the shotgun and jam it against the man's head. At that moment, he turned and saw me watching and realized what a horrible mistake he was about to make. Much to the crowd's disappointment, he said, "Let him go." With that, they turned the man loose. He staggered off and never came back.

I sincerely doubt I had as much to do with saving that man's life as Mom did, because I'm sure the whole time this was going on, she was in the house, on her knees, praying to God to keep Dad from committing murder. And He did!

The Savannah River garbage-filled swamp that Henry Schultz once proudly named "Hamburg," as we found it.

Birth of a Dream

I've been asked many times, as I've shared some of my war stories surrounding my involvement with the development of North Augusta's riverfront and the golf course that now sits proudly on the banks of the Savannah River: If I had it to do all over again, would I do it? My knee-jerk response is, "I don't know." I always hesitate to give a straight answer because of what I put my family through and the terrible price we all paid for chasing my dream.

No question about it: if it had involved only me, I'd do it all over again in a minute. Even now, I occasionally find myself chasing yet another dream, but that's another story. The reason I'd be willing to put myself through this whole ordeal again is not for some noble vision or the prospects of fortune and fame, or even for great community improvement. It would be simply for the awesome experience. That's where it's at, at least for me. How many people get an opportunity in life to "raise the dead?" At least, that's how I saw it—to have the privilege of reviving a significant piece of real estate where so much sweat, blood and tears lay just inches below the ground.

For 170 years this magnificent piece of God's creation had been carved up and styled into a proper village, suffered the destruction of war, deteriorated into a slum, was inundated in violent floodwaters, then left in ruins, parceled off, cut over, dug up, and the ultimate insult: dumped on. That's right: a garbage dump. The City of North Augusta had used a portion of the property for a city dump. Now I envisioned a unique opportunity to resurrect it.

That's a tremendous task for anyone, let alone a guy from Nellieville, where I got to know such interesting characters as Sticky Jack, Aunt Nellie, and Mr. Chin and his mule. And the lessons I learned there about the complexity of human behavior and the forces that drive it would be invaluable to me later in business. By contrast, in my professional career I would deal with people from all over the world, from backgrounds and cultures radically different from mine—some of them very much like me, and others from worlds I could never have imagined.

What made me think I was the one to pull this off in the first place, particularly when I didn't have two dimes to rub together and everyone was telling me it couldn't be done? To answer that question, a little history is necessary as to how I became acquainted with the property, or as my wife reminded me, married to it.

How does one become so passionate about a piece of ground that through no fault of its own became so ugly? It's as though the spirit of some ancient Indian medicine man or the ghost of Henry Schultz was the monkey on my back that wouldn't let me go, no matter how hard I tried.

What drove me to think I could do what others before me had tried to do and had given up on before they got out of the chute. Maybe it hinges on believing the words I heard my grandmother repeat many times—"where there's a will, there's a way"—or maybe it was daring to prove to others it could be done. Whatever the reason, the overriding one for me was the vision. There's a Bible verse that rings in my ears: "Without a vision, the people perish." It was my vision. I knew that the one and only path forward that made any sense, given its location in the flood plain and the wetlands restrictions that limited the land's ultimate potential, was a unique golf course designed to coexist with nature's beauty to create a totally memorable experience for the golfer.

When he was developing the town of Hamburg, Henry Schultz' vision was unencumbered by these modern-day restrictions, and as a result, the devastating destruction of flood waters in 1929 eventually brought the town's demise. Since then, it had been sitting there for over 55 years waiting for someone with the courage and the imagination to do something with it.

Mr. Knox, who many referred to as "Mr. Pete," owned the largest tract of land, which was 170 acres. He also had a vision for how the property should be developed, which he shared with me in the late 1980s. He unraveled an old, yellowed roll of drawings, which he was quite proud of, illustrating an elaborate theme park with amusement rides, lakes and trails. For some reason, he wanted my opinion of his master plan. I was reluctant to give it because I could see that Mr. Knox had paid good money for a plan that would not be successful in the local marketplace. However, I did express my concerns, and to my surprise, he agreed. He, too, thought it was over-the-top and somewhat out of place. I think it was at that point where we both gained respect for each other's opinions. Having nothing to lose, I unveiled my vision, which was a routing plan for an unusual 18-hole championship golf course that would stretch the full distance between the Thirteenth Street Bridge and Fifth Street Bridge.

After deliberating for a moment or two, Mr. Pete

agreed that there was some merit to my plan but noted
that a lot of additional outparcels would have to be
acquired to facilitate routing the holes around the existing lakes and wetlands. Evidently, Mr. Pete and several
of his associates had already tried to acquire some additional tracts, but were unsuccessful in their attempts. My
enthusiasm for what I knew was the ultimate land use
for the property trumped the thought that there would
be any problem acquiring these outparcels. My thinking
was flawed. I thought that reasonable landowners would
welcome the prospects of transforming the riverfront that
had been continually raped over the last 170 years. Boy,
was I wrong!

Given our history of working together on several
past projects such as converting Sacred Heart Cathedral
into Sacred Heart Cultural Center, renovating efforts
in Augusta's Olde Town and a couple of properties in
Thomson, Georgia, I was hoping that Mr. Knox, being
a well-heeled entrepreneur of some renown, might agree
to fund this project. I posed the question and Mr. Pete's
response wasn't what I wanted to hear. His comment to
me was "I'm too old to take on a project that's going to
take so long to develop. Why don't I sell you the property,
then you put it together and develop it." I knew that was
out of the question.

John Thomas, my business partner for over twenty
years and I had recently weathered a near financial disaster. Due to the recession of 1982, when interest rates hit
14-15%, we finally called it quits in the summer of 1988.
In light of that, knowing full well my responsibilities to
my family, I needed to find a way to make some money. I
was hoping Mr. Knox and I could work out some type of
financial arrangements to relieve this mounting financial
pressure, but my hopes were dashed when he suggested

that I buy the property. That was crazy, even if I wasn't in such a desperate situation. Where in the world would I find the money necessary, not only to purchase Mr. Pete's property, but also the outparcels? I thought he was playing me. He could probably see the desperation on my face, but what the heck? I decided to play the game and asked the next logical question, "How much?" Off the top of his head, without hesitation, Mr. Pete replied, "One million dollars." I felt a lump jump up in my throat, but I managed to retain my composure and keep my mouth shut. Besides, I wasn't in what you might call a very good negotiating position.

With hat in hand, I told Mr. Knox I'd have to think about it and get back to him. But what was there to think about? I was broke and didn't have a clue where my next dollar was coming from. I've learned that a nagging, gnawing knot in the pit of your stomach that won't go away is a good thing, particularly if you are a developer, or in my case, a wanna-be developer. I believe it's God's way of convincing you to proceed. It's sort of like meeting the girl of your dreams. To catch her, you have to pursue her. You can't get her off your mind. That's a little melodramatic, but that's how it works for me. If it's a good idea, it sticks. My wife, Brenda, knew about my meeting with Mr. Knox and my hopes of striking some type of deal, and her expectations weren't as optimistic as mine. When I told her Mr. Knox suggested I buy the property and that he wasn't remotely interested in a joint venture, she wasn't at all surprised. With a stiff upper lip, her piercing blue eyes holding back tears, she asked, "What are we going to do?" I replied, "I guess I'll take the job in Hilton Head."

Well after midnight, after our boys were asleep, I experienced one of life's defining moments — and it was an incident that would indeed alter the rest of my life. The old house we had just renovated was completely quiet and, laying next to each other in the still of the night, we must have talked for hours. Our faith had taught us that God has a plan for our lives. He controls it all, and we just have to trust Him. After living a life of vanity, Solomon put it this way: "It's the sole duty of man to live his life in the fear of God and to keep His commandments." As a believer, God's promise to never leave us or forsake us has proven to be true in my life, and I thank God for that every day. At this crucial turning point in our lives, a decision had to be made. We prayed about it, and asked God to give us the wisdom of Solomon.

Over the years I've discovered that women have been blessed with a couple of God-given senses that men don't possess: a high tolerance for pain and the ability to manage a budget. I know that to be true because the decision we made that night required both. Brenda had heard me talk about North Augusta's Riverfront for years and knew how passionate I was about my vision. Her head was most likely telling her one thing, but her heart was asking, "Why did I ever marry a dreamer in the first place?" We both knew that turning my vision of the river property into a reality was at best a long shot. Aside from the huge issues of finding money and assembling 22 outparcels, the questions still lingered: Would we be successful in obtaining the necessary wetland permits and zoning—and was the golf market there to support the concept?

Brenda knew the odds, yet she signed up to become a dreamer herself. We were both excited and at peace with our decision. Now all we needed was $1,000,000 to buy the property.

GETTING A DONE DEAL

Mr. Knox had stated his position in the usual straightforward manner: "One million dollars. That's the number, $5,882 per acre."

I knew from past experience that it is difficult to operate a financially successful golf course where land costs exceed $1 million. I also knew that Mr. Knox had that number fixed in his head, so to think I could negotiate some lower number was pure fantasy. What I also knew was that on the Augusta side of the River, about 200 yards away, plans and development were well underway for the Augusta Convention Center, Port Royal Condominiums, and there was talk of a Georgia Golf Hall of Fame being located within sight of the property. Several million had already been spent on constructing Riverwalk and the amphitheater, and with all that new construction being proposed, it didn't take a genius to realize the impact that investment would have on the property value and future success of the golf course.

On the North Augusta side of the river, there were the physical limitations of the flood plain to contend with. The wetlands would hamper potential building opportunities, and the ultimate success of the golf course would have to be market-driven. Of course, Mr. Knox was privy to this same information and had obviously decided to let fools rush in where angels feared to tread. In other words, maybe my enthusiasm and passion could melt the ice and make something good happen. I was sure that if I could get the ball rolling, it would be hard to stop.

The first and most crucial order of business was to get Mr. Pete's name on a contract. I called my attorney, Zack Everitt, who had been our corporate attorney for the past twenty years. Zack knew my history, and over the years we had developed a friendship that has lasted to this day. Zack, I imagine, is like most attorneys—not mincing words, he gets right to the point.

As I met with him to discuss putting together the contract, his question was, "What's the deal?" I recounted my conversation with Mr. Knox and that he had agreed to sell me the property for $1 million. In my thinking, if I were successful to get Mr. Knox to agree to my terms and conditions, I would then be in a position to attract investors to fund the project by selling an interest in the land contract.

Zack leaned back in his chair with his hands clasped behind his head and looked a little puzzled when I explained how I wanted the contract written. I wanted a two-year closing date and I wanted my work product to stand good for the earnest money deposit. Zack's first reaction was, "Why are you wasting my time? Mr. Knox will never go for that." So I suggested we include $100 earnest money deposit in the form of a personal check to make the contract valid and leave a little something behind so Mr. Knox wouldn't forget me.

As I remember it, I had some reservations about that check clearing the bank! It's amazing what a leap of faith and a $100 check can accomplish. The way I saw it, God expected me to do the possible and let Him handle the impossible. My responsibility was simply to complete the due diligence aspect of the project.

Some of the work product included paying for outside consultants to perform market studies, delineation and documentation of existing wetlands, ecological studies, testing soils and hazardous materials that had been deposited through dumping over the years, obtaining permits from the Corps of Engineers, Fish and Wildlife, City and County... and the list goes on. In all, I estimated the cost of determining the feasibility of the project would range between $150,000 and $175,000, which would stand good for the earnest money deposit. By this time, Zack realized I was serious and agreed to draft the purchase contract as outlined. His comment was "Let's run it up the flagpole and see what happens. It's worth a shot."

All the while this was going on, my partner John Thomas and I were in the process of winding down our business and liquidating our company's assets, which simply amounted to storing some furniture and office equipment. We both decided we would start freelancing from our homes: John would work from his living room, and I would cram all my stuff into an 8x10 attic room which would be my base of operations.

John and I had originally met while attending the University of Georgia in the early seventies. We graduated from the School of Environmental Design at about the same time, were both married and were veterans as well as brothers in the Christian faith. How John and I ever became partners still amazes me. It's true that opposites do attract, because we were at opposite ends of the pole. John saw active duty in Vietnam serving as a lieutenant in the Marine Corps and came home with a purple heart after stepping on a land mine. His talent was talking, and he was so skilled that he could convince Eskimos to buy ice water and count the cups at the same time. Always a master numbers cruncher, he clearly thought I had gone off the deep end when I mentioned that I had asked Zack to draw up the contract to present to Mr. Knox. Though he had always been the consummate optimist, he reiterated all the woes and how I was wasting my time pursuing the impossible task of assembling all 22 outparcels. "Hey, I know the odds," I said. "Do you want your name on this contract or not? That's all I want to know." John and I, over the course of growing a business, had many heated discussions, and I wasn't in the mood to have another one. As ex-business partners, our professional association was over. We had decided to pursue separate careers, but as friends and brothers who had walked through countless fires together for twenty years, if by God's providence we were to gain a successful outcome, I wanted John to be a part of it. I recall him saying in a rather flip manner, "Okay, put my name on it." So I did.

Unlike John, my military career was all stateside. I received a congratulations notification from Uncle Sam in 1967 and joined the Air Force on June 8 that same year. There are two dates a vet always remembers: the day he enlists and the day he is discharged. In retrospect, my military career as an illustrator was not too distinguished. My drawing talent had served me well in that, after basic training, I went directly to my first duty station as an apprentice to a medical illustrator at Kesler AF Base in Biloxi, Mississippi. While John and a lot of other guys were dodging bullets in Vietnam, I was knee-deep in anatomical study by day and developing my lesser-known talent as a singer to entertain the troops in local bars up and down the Gulf Coast by night.

I don't know how it is today, but in those days, pop music was in. I enjoyed singing it, and my buddies enjoyed drinking the booze. The way it worked was this: I would sing three or four songs in my four-song repertoire, collect the booze for free entertainment and move on down the line. I must have been pretty good at it, because I won several base and command level talent shows and competed in two world-wide "Top of The Blues" shows at Edwards AF Base and Wright Patterson. I think what I took away from my Air Force experience was confidence: I learned that simply making the effort—risking possible failure—is the critical first step in achieving anything.

John was right in his opinion of how daunting the task was before us, because it was a one-shot chance that depended totally on Mr. Knox's willingness to accept the terms and conditions of the purchase agreement. Several days later I went by Zack's office to pick up the contract, reviewed it, and immediately called Mr. Knox. I happened to catch him in Augusta, and he suggested meeting later in the afternoon at his downtown office. I knew the importance of this meeting and was hoping to come away with a signed contract, but I also knew Mr. Knox hadn't achieved his success by making dumb mistakes.

Well, there I was, sitting across from Mr. Knox. I felt like I was back in grammar school, sitting in the principal's office, waiting for one of us to break the silence. I'm sure Mr. Knox had been in this position many times and negotiating contracts for $1 million was his second nature. But it was my first rodeo. My hands were sweating and my knees were knocking, but at least I was smart enough to keep my mouth shut. I slid a copy of the contract across the table. He picked it up and began reviewing it. Nothing was said about the price. It was exactly what he had asked. "A two-year closing date? That's unheard of," he said. I suggested he continue reading. When he came to the due diligence items outlined in the contract, he replied, "That's great, but where's my earnest money?" I said, "It's in there," proceeding to explain my rationale for structuring the contract as presented. "First, look at the amount of time and due diligence required in order to determine if the proposed golf course concept is even possible." Each item was thoroughly presented as to its necessity along with the associated out-of-pocket costs that would have to be paid to outside consultants. I also presented a time-line that I thought was reasonable for completion. Mr. Knox then expressed his concern about the absence of earnest money. I assured him if we weren't successful in purchasing the property, the work items produced to date would become his property and provide future purchasers the necessary information to make a rapid decision and facilitate a short closing date. I think he agreed with me on that point even though he never expressed it. I don't know exactly what Mr. Knox was expecting, but from my perspective, I had nothing to negotiate with, other than talent and time. Any modification to the terms and conditions of the contract would send John and me packing, and the property would have to sit there for another 170 years.

Mr. Knox's closing remarks were, "I'll have to talk this over with my boys and get back to you." The expression on Mr. Knox's face gave no clue as to what he was thinking. He must have played a lot of poker, because he sure had a good poker face.

As it turned out, I would have to wait for several agonizing weeks before walking away with a signed contract. In the meantime, John and I would have to trust God to do the impossible. I was resigned to the fact that whatever the outcome, God's hand was in it.

Those two weeks crawled by, but I remained optimistic, convinced that Mr. Knox had caught my vision, which if successful, would be mutually beneficial in helping to revitalize downtown Augusta.

Days became weeks without a word—I was on a short fuse, and with financial pressures mounting, something had to give. During that eternity, I never strayed far from home so I could hear the phone ring. Suddenly it did. Mr. Knox asked if I would drop by his office so we could talk about the contract. With hopes renewed, I made a beeline for his office, thinking all the way there, "If he wants to talk, there's the possibility that he actually believes I'm not completely crazy. Otherwise, he could have just as easily told me to forget it over the phone."

So there I was again, like a schoolboy, sitting across from Mr. Knox. I don't know why he intimidated me so completely other than the fact that he was twice my age and a whole lot smarter. When he spoke, he certainly had my attention and, based on our previous business dealings, he also had my utter respect. I found him to be a man of integrity, serious about business and making an honest buck. But as Augustans could testify, he was also a community leader willing to invest his money and time to make Augusta a better place. Above all, he was a straight shooter: good or bad, he called it like he saw it. Whatever was about to take place, that contract with its favorable terms and conditions was a business deal, and at the end of the day Mr. Knox was expecting a $1 million payday. I wasn't asking him for any favors, and he knew very well that the odds were stacked. I remember going over all the due diligence items in the contract once more, and then Mr. Knox responding: "I've discussed this with my boys. They say I'm crazy for what I'm about to do, but I believe you might be able to pull it off." With that, he signed the contract, had it witnessed, and history was in the making.

Looking back on that auspicious occasion and all that has taken place since then—not only on that riverfront, but also to the City of North Augusta—I would say that

Mr. Knox's signature on that piece of paper was the vital spark needed to light the fire. What influenced him to take the risk with me I don't know, but lots of people living in North Augusta are sure glad he did.

I called Zack with the news. He advised me to take the contract to the Aiken County Courthouse to have it recorded so I could maintain my first position should someone try to go around me and steal the project. The 170 acres now under contract were strategically located between the Thirteenth and Fifth Street bridges, so having control over the largest land parcel gave me some comfort and advantage over land speculators that might be looking to make a quick buck.

There were 21 other parcels to acquire: the clock was ticking, and my personal financial situation was continuing to spiral downward.

John and I had always been able to resolve our differences. Anyone in a partnership knows there will be disagreements; but our unique conflict resolution process worked because we recognized and appreciated each other's strengths and weaknesses. While that mutual understanding helps, ultimately that isn't enough. Our policy had always been that the partner who discovered the project, put it together and had the client's confidence had the last word. Although we had dissolved our design firm, John and I agreed we would maintain that same approach as we moved forward, and I would take the lead. Yet, even with a signed contract in hand, John remained skeptical about the project.

There were several advantages in my taking the lead on this project: my golf course design experience working with George Cobb who designed the Par 3 at Augusta National; my eight years of service on the Planning and Zoning Commission of North Augusta; and my strong

community ties.

We saw both opportunities and obstacles ahead. Now all we could do was move forward, believing that somehow everything would work out.

SHOW ME THE MONEY

Getting Mr. Knox to sign that contract was no small achievement, but it was only our first hurdle. There were a lot more hurdles to come. Some we could see, and others we never saw coming. One thing we knew for sure from our past experience: he who controls the land controls the deal. It's just much harder to control the deal with no money in your pocket.

I had always anticipated that finding a financial partner to underwrite such an ambitious project would be a tough nut to crack. Believe it or not, it wasn't. Exactly two weeks after getting the contract signed, I trotted across the river and met with a gentleman by the name of Frank Beard.

I can't remember ever having met Mr. Beard or having had any previous business dealings with him. Maybe Zack thought there might be an opportunity there, but regardless, I arranged to meet him at his home on Milledge Road across from Augusta Country Club. I unfurled the illustrative master plan that had served me well in convincing Mr. Knox to gamble with me. Mr. Beard was so favorably impressed with my concept that he offered a proposal of his own, which I wasn't the least bit interested in. He offered to purchase our land contract with

Mr. Knox for $100,000 subject to the project's feasibility and me agreeing to relinquish the rights to design the golf course. I viewed that as nothing more than a 10% real estate commission. I knew he would end up coming to the same conclusion as Mr. Knox—that putting the additional parcels together would prove too difficult and require more effort and money than could be justified.

John and I certainly could have used the cash, but we would be placing our future in the hands of investors who would look at the bottom line only. What I gleaned from that meeting was validation that the concept was rock solid and I was on the right track. What Mr. Beard was proposing is "Heads I win, tails you lose." I had seen enough to know it was time to find another candidate who would be more appreciative of what we were bringing to the table.

Although the results of that meeting were somewhat disappointing, the clock was ticking. Several weeks had already transpired on the contract; and if the due diligent items were to be completed on schedule, I had to find a money partner, and fast. Who was out there who would benefit most from seeing this project move forward? I decided that it was the people who would view the golf course from the other side of the river: the people who had already invested millions, who had staked their claim on the Augusta side of the river in hopes of creating a high-end residential condo market. Our most logical move was to approach the Port Royal group, since the golf course would eventually be in their back yard.

Several years earlier Bennett-Murray-Thomas & Associates, our firm, had been retained by Dr. Theo Ballenger to design his medical office on Harper Street in Augusta. During the course of that project, Dr. Ballenger mentioned that his brother was a developer in Portugal and the two of them were planning to develop a project on the riverfront. He asked if our firm had any experience with high-rise construction and, from what he was describing, I knew it was beyond our expertise. He asked my opinion of the project but didn't offer enough information for me to give him an honest answer. The informal manner in which the question was asked and the sheer magnitude of what was being described made it hard for me to take him seriously.

As it turned out, I underestimated Dr. Ballenger's seriousness! He was quite serious, and evidence of his seriousness was already rising from the ground! The Port Royal project was approximately 20-30% complete. It occurred to me that the golf course would be a tremendous aid in their real estate marketing efforts and would complement their riverfront development concept beautifully. I knew Dr. Ballenger well enough to make a personal call and introduce him to my concept. Not only was he was interested—he asked that I call Ron Hodges, the head of the Port Royal Group to schedule a more formal presentation to his partners.

Ron and I knew each other from past experience when he was employed as Planning Director for the City of North Augusta and I was serving on the Planning Commission. Due to the nature of our careers, our paths had crossed frequently. We often discussed North Augusta's riverfront and the opportunity it held to put North Augusta on the map. These conversations were back in the mid-80s, but even then, popular opinion held that there was absolutely no way to assemble the properties without the use of the City's power of eminent domain. We knew that wasn't going to happen, both for political reasons and because of limitations that restricted the property to only public and recreational uses. Under that scenario, there wasn't much

PHOTO: ASHLEY BENNETT

*The Port Royal condominium project soars into the sky, a promi-
nent addition to the Augusta side of the Savannah River.*

opportunity for the City to broaden its tax base. That's
when I began to visualize how our riverfront could best be
developed despite its limitations.

Ron had moved on. I knew he was now involved with
the Port Royal Group from having seen his name quite
often in the Augusta Chronicle. We had lost contact over
the years, so I welcomed the opportunity to renew an old
acquaintance and share my latest thoughts and plans for
North Augusta's riverfront. I wasn't sure where this might
go, but I regarded Ron as a friend and knew he would be
sympathetic to what I was trying to do.

By the time the meeting took place at their attorney's
office, our presentation and exhibits were much more
polished. John was starting to warm up to the idea that
maybe I wasn't so crazy after all. I invited him along so he
could use his silver tongue, if necessary. Making presentations in our line of work was pretty common, and over the

years John and I got rather good at it. All our past experience must have paid off because we were successful in recruiting the Port Royal Group as our financial partner, forming a 50/50 partnership named Primrose.

The terms of the deal were simple. We gave the Port Royal Group a 50% interest in the land contract, and they were to provide the funds necessary to complete the due diligence work. Our new partners thought the foreign bank that was financing the Port Royal condo project might be interested in providing the long-term financing for our project as well. If not, based on the terms of our agreement, they would find other outside investors or alternate financing. It's not unusual for the group putting up the money to want controlling interest in a project or to become the general partner. John and I wouldn't have been too uncomfortable giving up the general partnership interest, but that wasn't necessary since we had only relinquished a 50% interest in the land contract and had confidence that we were all working in good faith to move the project forward.

The old adage applies, "He who has the gold, makes the rules." It's a hard lesson to learn, but when it comes to money, friendships don't count for much. It's easy to couch greed in the phrase, "It's just business!" In the movie "Wall Street" Gordon Gekko's mantra is "Greed is good." By contrast, the biblical apostle Paul equates greed with idolatry in his letters to the early Christian churches. Over the course of my involvement with this project, I confronted greed in every form imaginable, from the slick to the crude and everything in between. No surprise there... looking back, avarice has always been firmly rooted in the history of the riverfront.

It was exciting to have a money partner on board and feel an easing of some of the personal financial burden

John and I were carrying. Our agreement with Primrose allowed for Bennett/Thomas to receive compensation for design services related to completing the due diligence items outlined in the Knox contract and the coordination of outside consultant services. Completing the due diligence items was work, but they were things you could get a handle on—things like delineation of wetlands, market studies, soils investigations, and the like were things you could attack straight on: evaluate, make judgment calls and keep moving. That was the easy stuff. What wasn't easy, which is an understatement, was the land assemblage process. From the beginning I had realized that it would be difficult to put all the pieces together. I heard that sentiment from everybody, but I could never have anticipated what I was actually getting myself into.

My agreement with John allowed me to make the last call on all critical decisions of the project. After much discussion, we thought it best to let John deal with the project's engineering aspects and let me personally pursue the individual landowners. Knowing John's personality— primarily his Marine training and the fact that he lived on the opposite side of the River—predicted a battle we couldn't win in a respectful negotiation. I knew if even one landowner got upset and thought we were trying to take advantage of them, we were cooked. Although John would never do that intentionally, I was afraid the landowners would see him as an outsider and a heartless developer looking to strike it rich. My approach would be to look the landowners straight in the eyes, one-on-one, and gauge their reaction when I mentioned we were interested in purchasing their property on the River. We certainly were no Disney Corporation, nor did we have time to set up dummy corporations to buy the property. Besides, the word was already starting to leak out all over town that something was about to happen on the River.

My approach, right or wrong, was simple. It hinged on my belief that, for the most part, people aren't stupid and they do read the newspaper. My dad's admonition had always been equally simple: you don't lie, you don't cheat, and you don't steal. That was my approach—just be straightforward and honestly answer questions asked. My upbringing and my conscience wouldn't let me do it any other way.

I quickly learned that not all my landowners shared my straightforward values: their greed just got the better of them. Of course, there is a difference between greed and striking an exceptionally good deal—nothing's wrong with getting the best value you can. It's the American Way.

From the start, I had expected that the land purchases would be based on fair market appraisals. Although we hadn't closed on Mr. Knox's tract, it served as a good starting point for future negotiations—a guide that set the price around $5,000 to $8,000 per acre. After all, we're talking about land that was located in the 100-year flood plain. The only exception to that low-lying elevation was the Parks property, which was about a quarter of an acre set slap in the middle of my proposed golf course. It was absolutely necessary to acquire a purchase agreement on this tract first, because the Parks physically lived on the property and had an access easement from both ends of the site, which would make routing the holes around the golf course impossible.

It wouldn't make any sense to pursue the other tracts if we weren't successful in getting the Parks to sell. But that effort would prove to be well beyond anything I anticipated.

THE LAND PUZZLE

The Parks were an African-American family, and interestingly, the only remaining descendents of the black families that had once populated Hamburg following the Civil War. All my contacts with them had to be done in person because they didn't have a phone, and I remember my first visit quite vividly.

It was late afternoon and the shadows were growing long across a narrow, muddy road leading to their house. It was impossible to drive in, so I had to walk, continually jumping from one side of the road to the other in order to dodge the mud holes that led to their house. I was reminded of how thoughtless some people could be as I walked past trash and debris of all sorts dumped on each side of this "mud hole road" on such hallowed ground. If successful with our plans, we would inherit this mess and also the responsibility of cleaning it up.

As I continued to make my way toward the house, I could see that someone was at home. The house sat on a large clearing and was made of concrete blocks. Most of its green paint had peeled away, and the house showed evidence of much-needed repair. Kids in the yard saw me coming and called to the Parks that they had a visitor.

Mr. and Mrs. Parks met me at the door and invited me in. I introduced myself, making sure they knew I wasn't a bill collector. I said, "I suppose you don't have to worry about many visitors around here." Mr. Parks nodded affirmatively as I explained that I was interested in purchasing his property. I assured them that if they would be interested in selling, I would be willing to assist them in finding another place to live. I suggested we have the property appraised to determine its value. Then he commented that he wouldn't be interested in selling if he couldn't get at least $50K-$60K for the property. In the late 1980s, that was a reasonable amount of money, and I was pleased to come away with a number that I thought was a little high, but fair. That put the per acre price at about $200,000. The following morning I called Zack, told him about my visit, and asked him to draw up a purchase contract in the amount of $50,000.

Later that week, I picked up the contract and went up to Ron's office to get the earnest money deposit. I was stoked, to say the least, and eager to get the Parks to sign since this property really had the potential of making or breaking the project. My plan was to deliver it on Saturday when most folks aren't working—and I would walk out of there with a signed contract while the sun was still shining.

At that juncture, I thought I had done everything right. However, as I maneuvered my way on foot along the muddy road I had previously walked, I sensed something wrong. As I approached the clearing, there were several cars around the house and a lot more people. My first impression was that there must be a family reunion or some sort of party going on, and people were drinking and having a good time. What really got my attention was a hog hanging from a tree, gutted, and ready for barbeque.

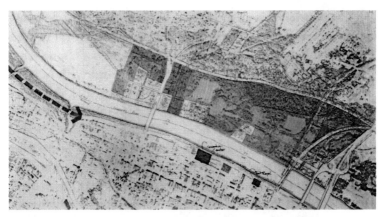

An early plat showing Mr. Knox's parcel and all the additional lots that would need to be secured to make the project happen.

I hadn't been invited, so I wanted to complete this business transaction as quickly as possible and get out of there.

The screen door was wide open and pressed back against the wall. Mrs. Parks met me as I was walking up and invited me in. To my surprise, there was Mr. Parks stretched out on the couch, eyes and mouth wide open, saying not a word. On my first visit, Mrs. Parks hadn't had much to say. She was even quieter on this occasion, quite understandably for she was distressed by her husband's condition. She told me that Mr. Parks had suffered a stroke a few days earlier; therefore, any further conversations about purchasing the property would have to involve her son. She went on say that her son was a sergeant in the Air Force, stationed at Robins Air Force Base in Warner Robins, Georgia. As she gave me the information on how to contact him, I got the eerie feeling that things had just made a turn for the worse.

It took me several weeks to finally contact Parks, Jr. I was anxious to meet with him and review the terms of the contract his father and I had previously discussed.

On the drive over to Robins (a drive I had made many times before since it was my last duty station before my Air Force discharge in 1971) I thought there was a chance that Parks, Jr. and I might have a common bond with our Air Force connection. Although I was hoping that the price and terms of the agreement I had previously discussed with his father would be honored, I had anticipated that there may be some slight price change and was more than willing to have the property appraised to determine the fair market value. But what I encountered was an attitude that would set the trend for other future land acquisitions.

If my thinking had been naïve, I was quickly shocked back to reality when he announced his take it or leave it price: $250,000. With a sudden, almost audible screech, the brakes had just stopped my vision cold in its tracks. I knew right then that when it comes to land, nobody gives a hoot about anything but money. What I didn't know was that this was only Act One; there would be 20 acts left to follow, each orchestrated with the underlying theme of greed.

My jaw dropped to the floor and I told Parks, "You're talking about a quarter of an acre of land. That equals $1 million per acre. I have a contract with Mr. Knox to purchase 170 acres for $5,800 per acre. This doesn't make any sense." His attitude was firm. I decided to leave it and fight that battle another day. Besides, I couldn't recommend paying that amount of money even if my new partners agreed to it. Parks was holding all the cards, and he knew it. I had no leverage—all I could do was leave my name and number and hope to hear from him in the near future.

There was absolutely no purpose in worrying over something we couldn't control, so John and I continued coordinating and contracting with outside consultants to complete the remaining work items. Just like the land

acquisition process, we prioritized those items by considering the impact they would have on the physical and
financial feasibility of the project. We placed supreme
importance on the financial success of the golf course. If
the demand for play wasn't there, we needed to pull the
plug and all bets were off.

Of course, that language was in the contract with Mr.
Knox, who understood the importance of documenting the
project's feasibility if we were to be successful in securing
long-term financing. We contracted with Golf Resources,
a firm in Atlanta that specialized in evaluating current
golf market conditions in order to assess the likelihood of
the golf course's success. Golf Resources then arranged
for a rather elderly gentleman from Florida to inventory
the existing golf courses in our area and document their
potential impact on our proposed course.

Before getting started, this gentleman wanted to meet
with me, orient himself to the area, and have me show
him the location of our proposed course. The best vantage
point to appreciate our location was from the Augusta
side of the River. As we stood near the amphitheater
gazing across the river, the old man asked the question,
"Where's the golf course going to be located?" I pointed to
the Thirteenth Street Bridge and then turned and pointed
to the Fifth Street Bridge. I told him it was all the land
between the two bridges. I can't remember his name, but
I will never forget the old man's reaction: surprise and
astonishment permeated his face. Incredulous, he asked,
"You mean to tell me you control all that land?" I replied,
"That's the plan." He looked at me and said, "Son, you
don't need a market study. With a location like this, you
surely don't need a market study."

To have a professional and an outsider view the property for the first time and have a reaction like that fueled

my fire. Later that day before leaving, the old man wanted to meet briefly with me to recap the events of his day. He made another comment that I found rather amusing and that only Augustans can appreciate. He said, "Son, I've seen a lot of golf courses in my day, but what I've discovered about Augusta, Georgia is that you have the best golf course in the world (referring to the Augusta National) and you also have the worst golf course I've ever seen" (referring to the Augusta Municipal Golf Course, nicknamed the Cabbage Patch.)

The Cabbage Patch might be the worst, but it holds fond memories for me. It's where I made my golfing debut after sarcastically commenting on my Dad's golfing ability.

In the early 1960s, Dad had open heart surgery to have a valve replaced. After recovery, doctors recommended he take up the game of golf for physical therapy. He recruited me to be his caddy. It seemed like every Sunday afternoon we would walk 18 holes with me pulling the cart all around the course, and that was getting old quickly. Because of my dad's physical condition, he could only make a three-quarter back swing at best, which limited his ability to score. On one occasion I made a comment that he didn't appreciate: "Dad, I don't understand why you play golf—you always score the same, between 90-92, so why bother playing?" He didn't take my comment as constructive criticism, so he said, "If you think you can do better, you try it." So I did. Since then, I've played many different golf courses, broken par a few times, had a hole in one, played the Augusta National on several occasions, and even worked with a couple of golf celebrities on golf course designs.

Be that as it may, my two most memorable golf outings were with my father at the Cabbage Patch. The first 18 holes I ever played was Christmas Day when I got a driver, 5 irons and a putter. It was a day my dad got even with me for that catty remark about his game. It was embarrassing to say the least, and dad made sure that every stroke was counted—no mulligans, a whiff was a stroke, no moving the ball: we played by the rules. By the end of the round, I needed a calculator to add all those 2-digit numbers. To this day I've tried to forget it—169, that's the number. As I've learned over the years, golfers are always looking for an excuse: backache, bad lies, sun in the eyes, whatever. The only one I can come up with is the fact that I'm left-handed. I bat left-handed and do everything left-handed but play golf. Dad wouldn't let me play left-handed. That's a new one, and it's an excuse that ranks up there with the best of them.

The one outing I cherish the most was again at the Patch playing with my dad, and this time, he was the caddy. Through much practice, I had improved so quickly that within a year I was playing well enough to be facing my final opponent to win first flight in a Budweiser tournament.

My final opponent was an elderly gentleman who had a good game but was short on conversation. After several holes, I was beginning to question what was going on. I was getting murdered and couldn't stop the bleeding. I tried, but couldn't find my swing, and my attitude was starting to show my frustration. Dad was sort of like me— he couldn't figure out what was going on either, but would offer a word of encouragement now and then, which only made things worse. At the end of nine holes, I was nine holes down. With only nine holes left to play I was ready to throw in the towel and forfeit the match. That's when I discovered a new side of my father. I was ready to walk to the car when he said, "Where do you think you're going?" I tried to explain that I couldn't beat this guy because he was better and more experienced than I. My dad said, "I don't give a damn if he beats you or not, but you're not quitting. You're gonna finish."

I knew when my Dad's face got red he was serious, and quitting wasn't a word in his vocabulary. The 10th hole at the Patch was a short par three surrounded by bunkers on both sides. Somehow I managed to get out of there with a par, win the hole and succeeded to win each hole thereafter. At the end of 18 holes, the match was even. Neither my opponent nor my father could believe what had transpired. It was amazing! The final outcome of the match would have to be decided in a sudden death playoff, starting at hole #1.

I had the momentum and was confident the match was mine for the taking. I was on the green in three—all I needed was to 2 putt and the "green jacket" was mine. I had about a 20-foot putt left for a birdie and a perfect lie, but forgot to hit it, leaving me with a four-foot knee knocker. The second putt was uglier than the first. It was a straight in putt, but I pulled it, lipping the left side of the cup. Dad assured me we would get him on the next hole, a par 4 downhill. I was still determined I could beat this guy even though I had missed a golden opportunity to polish him off on the previous hole. What happened next is the essence of telling this story. Playing golf is a lot like life— just when you think you've got it figured out, it throws you a curve. It's how you handle those curves that tests the mettle of who you are and defines the stuff you're made of.

Let me tell you how the match ended and you'll get the picture: it was a par 4 hole and I was on the green in 2 with another 25-foot putt left to make birdie. My opponent had hit his drive into the woods and was struggling to find the fairway, which he did with his second shot, leaving 40-50 yards from the green. The obvious way this match should have played out was for my opponent to be on the green in three, and most likely two-putt for a bogie five. I would then be in a position to two-putt for a par and win the match, but it didn't work out that way. Who would have ever have thought my opponent would knock his third shot in the hole from 50 yards out, especially when he hit a worm burner crawling all the way into the hole?

At the moment, the wind left my sail. My opponent went completely bonkers, running around the fairway, hollering, jumping up and down. All he needed was fireworks to let everyone on the course know that he had just won the match. I missed my birdie putt, and the match was over. No excuses—that's golf, that's life.

What I took away from that experience was a newfound respect for my dad. He was no quitter, a man of few words, hard, short-tempered and not given to expressing his feelings. I never once in my entire life heard him use the word 'love.' I think he felt it, he just couldn't say it. What I felt and heard on this particular occasion as we walked back to the car were words of consolation and praise that was so out of character for my father. I think we both gained some respect for each other. The love was felt, but not spoken.

Because, of his insistence, I learned the true meaning of being a winner. I have to give Dad credit for that—even though I didn't win the match, I had won self respect, knowing I had given it my all. I found new meaning in all the clichés: A quitter never wins; It's not if you win or lose, but how you play the game that counts; Sometimes you win, sometimes you lose, sometimes you get rained out. I was truly a winner that day. No trophy, but I had my dad's respect and a newfound confidence that I would never know what I could accomplish unless I try. That lesson has served me well through life.

On April 7, 1963 My dad's last wish was granted when, at age 50, he died suddenly of a heart attack while lining up a putt at Green Meadows Country Club. That day was also the day 23 year-old Jack Nicklaus donned his very first green jacket at the 27th Masters Tournament.

I'm getting a little philosophical, but while I'm on the subject, another personal lesson I've learned from playing this crazy game of golf is that it does matter how you play the game. In an era when so much emphasis is placed on winning, we sometimes forget why we play the game in the first place. Where's the glory in cheating, lying or scheming? Winning at any cost is self-defeating, ultimately taking a toll on one's self-esteem and destroying personal integrity. There a proverb that says, "A good name is to be treasured more than rubies," so where's the glory in winning at any cost? I know this flies in the face of modern day thinking, but I would rather lose with my head up, knowing I've played by the rules; rather than win at any cost, I would give it my all, and know with practice I'll get better. By cheating all the way to the top in order to win, I would have to continually deny my conscience, knowing how I got there.

The consultant, when he made those derogatory remarks about the "Patch," wasn't aware that he had hit a nerve. It was an off-the-cuff remark, of course, and was taken as such. To set the record straight—since then, I've been employed as a golf course consultant by the National Golf Foundation on numerous occasions to perform similar assignments across the southeast, and I can assure you I've seen a whole lot worse.

Another critical area of concern, second only to the strength of the golf market, was the impact of wetlands. In order to successfully route the individual holes around the site, it was necessary to expand some areas by adding fill material in the wetlands, creating new high ground. The Army Corps of Engineers out of the Charleston District had jurisdictional authority over issuing permits for this; but the Corps worked in conjunction with the U.S. Fish and Wildlife Commission, which had to sign off on environmental issues, such as endangered species and loss of habitats. Without their OK, the Corps of Engineers wouldn't issue a permit. Another requirement was that elements of archeological significance that might be discovered during construction could not be exposed to daylight. These artifacts were not to be uncovered, but should remain in place for future generations to discover. Fill material could be placed over the top of them, but cutting or removing soil was prohibited.

It was highly advantageous for us to obtain what's known as a Nationwide 26 Permit, which allowed impacting up to ten acres and gaining approval in the least amount of time, usually within thirty days. Otherwise we would be forced to obtain a full-blown permit which, in some cases, can take years to obtain with no guarantee of a successful outcome. Our contract with Mr. Knox didn't give us the luxury of time, so it was critical that the golf course be routed in a manner that created minimal impact by working toward securing a National 26 Permit. I would interject that, working under today's requirements, obtaining a nationwide permit would be impossible. In the 1990s, ten acres were the allowable impacts; today's impacts in excess of .1 of an acre, 4,356 square feet, require a full-blown permit which takes time and money. In total, after many course routing alternatives had been explored, we ended up impacting about 7 acres of wetlands which we worked extremely hard to achieve.

We contracted with a firm from Summerville, SC, who had a good rapport with the Corps of Engineers, to

PHOTO: ASHLEY BENNETT

Snakes and alligators made this land their favored habitat and have no intention of giving it up.

delineate all the wetlands onsite. They sent a young college intern who worked for several days tramping over every inch of the property. He would start early in the morning, dressed in a long-sleeve shirt and thick jeans, with snake boots and leggings strapped around his legs. We wouldn't see him again until the sun went down, when he would come crawling out of the thicket. His face and arms dripped with blood from briar snags as he methodically placed blue flags outlining all the wetland perimeters. I knew what we were paying these guys and I thought to myself it wasn't enough. I remember asking the young man whether he had worked on other sites as difficult as this one. As he continually tried to stop the bleeding, he responded, "I haven't. This is absolutely the worst." I learned later that he decided to pursue a different career field.

Not only did the existing wetlands have to be delineated—they would also have to be surveyed as to their exact location. We contracted with Tripp McKie, a local surveyor with whom we had prior experience. Although Tripp was a one-man firm, we always found him to be competent and reliable.

I recall on one occasion that Tripp had some questions interpreting a flagging arrangement on the northeast corner of the property and asked for my assistance in sorting it out. I was happy to oblige and proceeded to put on my snake boots before we started tromping through the briars and underbrush. I had walked the property during the winter when snakes weren't a concern, but here in the heat of the summer, that was a horse of a different color. As we continued walking, the vegetation became more and more dense as we fought our way through. We came to a spot where we had to wade across a muddy marsh with embankments to the front and rear. By this time, Tripp was already several yards in front of me when I stopped dead in my tracks as I was looking straight into the eyes of a water moccasin, coiled and ready to strike. I turned, looking for an exit, and noticed another moccasin guarding my exit. My heart skipped a couple of beats, and I hollered to Tripp, "I'm getting the hell out of here!" and I did. I blazed a new trail, realizing this was no place for a Boy Scout. Eventually Tripp accomplished his mission, but not without some choice words as to what we had gotten him into. The property was a mess.

Another step in securing the required permits was having the US Fish and Wildlife Commission sign off on our plans detailing where wetland impacts were to be placed. The Corps of Engineers would be the agency issuing the permit, but would do so only when Fish and Wildlife had substantiated that minimum damage would be done to wildlife habitats. It made no difference to them that so much debris and garbage had already destroyed acres and acres of wetlands and wildlife habitat over the years. They were not interested in aesthetics or our beautification program, potential job creation, or expanding the tax base. Their job was to protect wetlands and habitat, which was okay by us, but don't tell me that getting rid of all that garbage is destroying habitat. I'm sure that a few rats and snakes were buried in that stuff, but in my way of thinking, they weren't an endangered species, so they would just have to pull up stakes and find a new home. Their squatter rights had just expired.

On the first visit by the Fish and Wildlife Commission, I met an agent early one hot summer morning. He drove in via the 13th Street Bridge, what is now called Clubhouse Drive. He had no sooner stepped out of his car when he saw an egret light in the top of a dead tree. His immediate comment to me was, "I hope you're not planning to have a golf hole where that tree's located." I unrolled my concept plan and noted the approximate location of the tree in question. It was located in an area that necessitated re-routing the hole. That one lone egret in that dead tree forced me to re-route the golf course several times. I disagreed with the agent's reasoning: he thought the tree was a nesting site for the bird. I didn't see how that could be possible, since the tree didn't have any limbs on it. The only way that bird could have built a nest in that tree was with hammer and nails. Nevertheless, the man had authority, so we played by his rules. Eventually we came up with a plan that minimized both the wetland impacts and saved the dead tree in the process.

Simultaneously, while working on securing the necessary permits, I continued contacting all the other surrounding landowners in an effort to establish a personal relationship, sending out letters of introduction to let each one know our interest in purchasing their property on the River. I wanted to break the ice—test the waters and get their response to see if they would even entertain an offer, let alone sell the property. I don't mean to belabor this point, because some of the land acquisitions were straight-

Photo: Ashley Bennett

forward and closed without a hitch. Some were typical in that there was much negotiation back and forth, arriving at a purchase price that was favorable to the landowner in almost every case. Then there were those who wouldn't give you the time of day. They were rude and downright impolite, putting it mildly—they were the ones that Mr. Knox and his agents had already encountered. Understandably, Knox had passed the baton over to an enthusiastic greenhorn, who just happened to be me.

Besides the Parks, there was another 14-acre tract that was crucial to acquire in order to facilitate positioning all 18 holes around the property. I had explored every possible alternative, reversing the routing, shortening and lengthening the holes, all to no avail. We had to have it. No response had been received from my initial introduction letter. Sooner or later I would have to make a personal contact with the owner. I thought I would just pick up the phone and give her a call.

I had never met this lady, so it was a cold call and I didn't know exactly what to expect. However, I've found most people to be reasonably polite unless your call interrupts a meal, which I always made sure I never did. The phone rang several times. I was anticipating hearing a soft, pleasant voice on the other end when she answered. What I heard was a hard-crass hello. From the tone of her voice, I realized this might be a short conversation. I managed to get out six words, "Mrs. Cochran, this is Mark Bennett," when, she replied abruptly, "Mr. Bennett, I know who you are, and don't ever call my house again." I may have gotten out only one more word, "But...", as she slammed the phone down in my ear. I'm glad I was sitting down, because I had never experienced such rudeness, not even in my courting days. I asked myself, "What did I ever do to this woman that would elicit such animosity?"

So much was riding on that single phone call. The riverfront's ultimate outcome could have ended right then and there with that brief, one-sided conversation. I was devastated and started to get the picture as to why this land had sat dormant for 170 years. Nevertheless, I was determined I wouldn't take no for an answer, particularly when I had worked so hard to persuade other people to invest not only in my vision, but also in me.

Even though my first encounter with Mrs. Cochran was not even close to what I had hoped for, I decided to give her the benefit of the doubt. Maybe she was just having a bad day or something, so a couple of weeks later I tried calling her again. This time, no sooner than my name was out of my mouth, I heard those familiar words, "Don't ever call my house again," and again the angry hang-up. At this point, I was starting to get the idea that she didn't want me to call her anymore... ya think?

There was only one thing left to do. That was to pay her a personal visit. The question was how was I going to do that without getting shot. I knew she would shut the door in my face: but it's strange how God intervenes when you don't know where else to turn. Some people would call it fate, but I disagree, and here's why: a day or so later I was cutting grass in my front yard when I saw Mrs. Baynham, my neighbor across the street. We struck up a casual conversation the way neighbors sometimes do. She asked how things were going with my project on the River since it had now become public knowledge through the local papers. I replied, "Not well at all," and went on to relate the difficulties I was having in assembling the properties. She reminded me that she also had property on the River, which I was aware of, and asked if I would be interested in purchasing it. Unfortunately, it was on the west side of the 13th Street Bridge and was not targeted as a high priority parcel. But during the course of that conversation, I asked Mrs. Baynham if she knew Mrs. Cochran, and she replied, "Yes, we play bridge together on Tuesday mornings. I know her quite well." I sensed from the conversation that Mrs. Baynham knew more about Mrs. Cochran than she was willing to say. Knowing she was much too fine a lady to gossip, I let it go at that. She did tell me that her son, Craig (ex-player for the Dallas Cowboys) was now a preacher and just happened to be Mrs. Cochran's pastor. She suggested I call Craig to see if he could help.

When he came by several days later, I told him what had happened when I tried contacting Mrs. Cochran by phone. I asked him to introduce me to her; of course, I knew this was an unusual request and suggested that if he felt uncomfortable intervening, I would understand. I would find another way to contact her. He offered his help but made no promises that he would be successful in arranging the meeting. Well, Craig was successful, and we met in Mrs. Cochran's house on Butler Avenue in North Augusta. That meeting took place 19 years ago as the three of us sat around a dimly lit kitchen table. The appearance of that house is still vividly etched in my brain, maybe because of the way the whole thing played out in the end.

Being the eternal optimist, I already had Zack draw up a purchase agreement leaving blanks for the purchase price and date. As it turned out, we never got that far.

What I did get from that meeting was an agreement, not signed, and not necessarily to my liking. But it was a verbal agreement made in front of and witnessed by her pastor. Mrs. Cochran stated in her own words, that if I was successful in acquiring all the other surrounding 20 parcels, she would sell me her fourteen acres. Maybe she didn't think it could be done, or maybe she was being wily as a fox. Whichever it was, all I wanted to know was that she would sell and that the purchase price would be reasonable. After all, 50% of her property was delineated as wetlands. Before Craig and I left, Mrs. Cochran assured me she would be fair-minded in placing a final price on the property, assuming I could assemble all the other tracts.

Looking back, I don't know what I could have done differently. I would have felt more comfortable if I could have gotten something in writing, but I knew from my previous one-sided phone conversation, that if I pushed her too hard, Lord knows what she would have done. All I could do for now was to take her at her word and hope and pray for the best. Craig said he thought the meeting went as well as could be expected, but as with his mother, I got the feeling there was something I wasn't being told. The Baynhams are great folks, and I was and am still very appreciative of their willingness to intervene in that situation. I can't say the same for the Mrs. Cochran. As unchristian as this may sound, she was an old biddy and that was the nicest thing I could say about her. Normally I take people at their word and believe that they mean what they say. As I learned later, much later, after assembling all the other tracts, truth was never in the equation. My gut feeling was that this woman couldn't be trusted, and she eventually proved me right.

As this tale unfolds, you will no doubt read between the lines that truth and honesty were in short supply and were by no means limited to my dealings with Mrs. Cochran. Let me assure you, I don't have a corner on those virtues, but what I've learned when doing a deal, regardless of its size, whether in business or in life, trust and negotiating in good faith is essential or the deal will ultimately fall apart.

By now we were three to four months into the project, and progress was being made on all fronts. We had confirmation from our golf market consultant that the market was there, subject to a quality course being constructed. Shortly thereafter, we were successful in finalizing negotiations with the Parks and contracted to purchase this strategically-placed property for $190,000, which was somewhat better than the $250,000 originally asked. Out of all the parcels we eventually purchased, I had no remorse about this purchase. We desperately needed this property, and they desperately needed a place to live, particularly in light of Mr. Parks' medical condition. After several trips back and forth to Charleston, our efforts to negotiate a compromise on wetlands impacts finally paid off. It was a happy day when I received our wetland permit, knowing we could successfully route the individual golf holes around the property in a way that was both playable and challenging. Things were really starting to come together, and for the first time, John, my partner, was starting to come around. From my perspective, things were going great, and it was an exciting time.

Whatever was good for John and me was also good for the Port Royal group, and rightly so. We constantly kept them in the loop and provided the necessary funds to keep things moving, as outlined in our 50/50 partnership agreement. I considered all of us friends as well as partners because of our past history.

However, on one occasion while meeting with my friend Ron Hodges with the Port Royal group, Ron made

One of our first conceptual renderings, with Port Royal Group as partners, was this Biarritz Golf Links master plan.

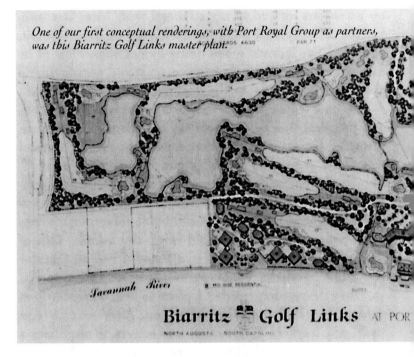

a startling statement: the terms of the agreement were about to change. Note that he didn't ask me to consider changing the terms of the agreement—he told me they were changing. I can recall his exact words: "Mark, we want 60-65% of the deal for ourselves." I asked how he could justify that. He replied, "I don't have to justify it, that's just the way it is." I was dumbfounded. I couldn't believe what I was hearing. This was completely out of the blue. Some 20 years later, his next remark still rings in my ears: "You need to put that in your pipe and smoke it." With that, I lost my religion and completely forgot the proverb about holding your tongue: I told Ron in a rather emphatic manner to just kiss my ass, because that was not going to happen. The way I saw it, this was my deal. I brought it to them and I wasn't about to let them screw

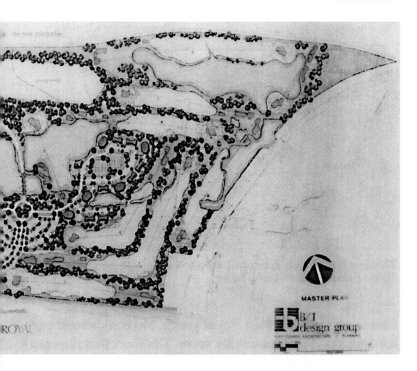

MASTER PLAN

B/I
design group

ROYAL

it up. At that moment, I lost complete confidence in my partners and would rather see the property just sit there for another 170 years than to yield to their greed.

Needless to say, the old golden rule, not the one in the Bible, but the other one that says, "He who has the gold, makes the rules" was in play. The problem was that I was not interested in playing. Once they showed their hand, it was over. Even if I wanted to, I couldn't muster the enthusiasm and the perseverance it would take to push the project forward while working with people I didn't respect or trust.

That day was a downer, and things were about to get a lot harder for John and me and our families. The money stopped, work stopped, fees stopped—it all stopped. For three to four months, little or no communication transpired

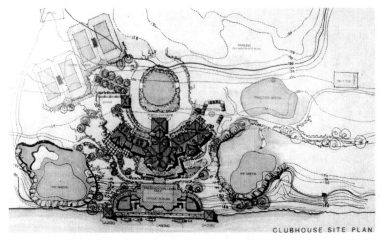

CLUBHOUSE SITE PLAN

The Biarritz Clubhouse, as designed, was positioned on a promontory overlooking the Savannah River directly below.

between us and the Port Royal group. Between a rock and hard place—that's where we were. The Port Royal group was just going to wait us out, and they certainly were in a financial position to do so. But I believe God hears our prayers, and I know for a fact that a lot of people were praying for us. That's the only explanation I have for the events that were about to follow.

The conversation I had months before with Mr. Knox, when we both shared our vision for the property, had now taken on a life of its own. You might say that in some small way we had let the genie out of the bottle. In other words, lots of folks had seen the concept and were starting to buy into the idea that it just might be doable. Sure, there were still a lot of land mines out there, particularly other key land acquisitions, but the word was out—something was about to happen on our riverfront.

Due to our standoff with Ron and the Port Royal group, we were put in a situation where we had to make something happen to get the project back on course. What that something was, we didn't have a clue. All I remember doing during the silent period was praying a lot and trusting that God had not let us get this far to fail. It's hard work to keep the faith, to believe that something good will come out of a desperate situation. But good did prevail, and we had absolutely nothing to do with it.

When we entered the agreement with Port Royal, it was in everyone's best interest to keep the lid on the project, knowing if word starting leaking out that it would complicate our land acquisition process and drive up land costs. The Port Royal group understood this from the beginning, but found it was advantageous in their marketing and sales efforts to use the Augusta Chronicle to promote our golf course across the river as part of their condominium project in Augusta. This may have helped them with their marketing effort, but as expected, it put all the landowners on alert and made dealing with them extremely difficult.

As John and I scratched our heads trying to figure out how to get the project out of stalemate, I received a phone call from Mel Story, a friend who had gotten out of the banking business and turned realtor. Mel had just listed two of North Augusta's most prized historical homes, and some out of town investors were interested in purchasing them. The houses were to be a part of a bed and breakfast chain with locations across the Southeast. Mel informed me that his purchasers had seen an article in the Augusta Chronicle about the proposed golf course and asked whether he knew the developers. That's why he called and asked if I would be available to meet with them later that afternoon, which I did.

The results of that initial meeting would change everything.

ENTER THE DRAGON

It's amazing how God opens some doors and closes others. I originally thought that when we signed the deal with Port Royal it would be a long-term relationship and we would all honor the terms of the agreement. We were unaware of the fact that the Port Royal Group wanted total control. John and I would have probably gone along with them if we had negotiated those terms in the beginning—but don't go changing the rules in the middle of the game for no apparent reason other than the obvious one: greed.

Little did we know that God was about to open another door which would not only change the course of the project but also the course of our lives. Let's face it: life is complicated. This ambitious project was complicated, but sometimes, particularly when your hands are tied and your back is against the wall, you just have to trust God and let go. I wasn't sure what was about to come out of this meeting with Mel Story and his investors, but for sure I welcomed the opportunity and was hoping for the best.

We met a little later that afternoon at the old Alexander mansion, which was one of the homes being considered by Mel's investors for purchase. As I was parking my car beside the house, I could see Mel and three distinguished-looking gentlemen walking around the grounds checking out this classic piece of real estate that was a significant part of North Augusta's history. I joined them and was casually introduced to John and Nobu Conyngham and Glenn McKinney, who was Hank McKinney's brother and architect for the group. Together, we continued the physical inspection of the property and concluded the tour on the front veranda , where I was given an opportunity to discuss my general overall concept for the golf course.

It took me about twenty seconds to realize that these guys were for real, as they shared their proposed renovation plans for the bed and breakfast inn. Too, I realized that John Conyngham, the spokesman for the group, was not your typical run-of-the-mill developer. Maybe it was his English accent or his age and personal charisma, but he impressed me as a gentleman with unusual intellect and character. Mr. Conyngham's interest in the golf course was quite simple: he thought his patrons, mostly foreign visitors, would enjoy having playing privileges at a local golf course in close proximity to the inn.

At this initial meeting, Mr. Conyngham mentioned he had an associate in Japan who owned and operated several golf courses overseas, who might be interested in becoming an investor in the river course. He said that on his upcoming trip to Japan, he would mention the course to his friend and invite him to come to North Augusta to view the project. The prospect of something happening to get the project back on track was exciting, but in reality, I knew it was another long shot.

Looking back, it is interesting to note that I didn't go looking for these guys. They had heard about the project through a newspaper article that, in my opinion, should never have been released. Obviously, whatever happened at this point was out of my control—but God works in mysterious ways. My grandmother always assured me that our ways are not His ways, but His ways are for our good and our benefit, if we will only trust Him.

Regardless of the friction that still lingered between me and Port Royal, it was incumbent on me to make them aware of the fact that we had a foreign investor group interested in participating in our project. I called Ron and informed him of our meeting and told him I would keep him abreast if anything materialized from their interest.

Several weeks later I received a call from Mr. Conyngham asking to schedule a meeting between us and several gentlemen from Japan to view the project. This was certainly great news, and to have investors come half-way around the world to view our project caused me some apprehension about exactly what they would see.

Unfortunately, I knew what they would see: the good, the bad and the ugly—and believe me, there was a lot of ugly. My goal was to get them to the point where they see more of the good. I knew if they arrived at the property from my normal entry point, their first impression would be a complete turn-off. Their first and maybe last impression would be the massive landfill that we would all have to wade through before seeing anything that smacked of potential beauty. I knew this mess had to be cleaned up and it wouldn't be cheap: we already had an estimate of $380,000 to do the job.

I wasn't trying to hide the fact that we had a landfill issue—we could see and discuss those issues on the way out. But I certainly didn't want their first impression to be a negative one, so my objective was clear: get them as close to the river as possible, then move toward the center of the property to a strategic vantage point we were proposing as the clubhouse location. From that location they would see the transformation happening across the river as Augusta continued its revitalization efforts. In order to make this favorable impression possible, a new entrance path had to be cleared, and that process would extract the last ounce of cash that John and I had. Believe me, that takes faith. Nevertheless, I remained confident that these were serious investors and believed in my heart of hearts that if we could just get them to the exact spot that had lit my fire years earlier, they would not be disappointed.

Well, it worked out exactly as planned. You've heard it said, "build it and they will come." In this instance, we built it... and they came. We went tracking through the woods with an entourage of Mr. Conyngham, Nobu, Glenn McKinney, our potential investor, Mr. Tanaka and his companions, and of course, John and I. You would not have believed all the commotion and the clamoring to try to communicate with each other as we grew closer and closer to our prepared viewing area.

When we arrived, you would have thought we had reached the Promised Land. The scene is hard to describe, because I didn't understand a single word that was said, but I could tell by their facial expressions and the excitement in their voices that they liked what they saw. I don't recall much conversation about Mr. Tanaka's interest level at this initial meeting. I think the culture shock and our earnest attempts to make a favorable impression were the order of the day.

The project by this time stood on its own merits: I knew it would sell itself if shown in the right light. Mr. Conyngham, as always, was very cordial and seemed very pleased that we had gone out of our way to make Mr. Tanaka and his associates welcome. Things could not have gone better. Mr. Tanaka and I seemed to hit it off, in spite of the fact that he spoke very little English. The only word I could speak was "hi" which translates as "yes." We spent most of that afternoon bowing, and when we couldn't figure out what the other person was trying to say, "hi" seemed to be the appropriate response. There was a lot of that, but through it all, with Mr. Conyngham's help in translating, Mr. Tanaka and I gained a mutual respect for each other connected through our passion for golf.

All I knew about Mr. Tanaka at this time was that he was a golf course entrepreneur in Japan who owned several courses there. I was told that he was now in the process of building another golf course where literally a mountain was being pushed into the ocean to create the course. It wasn't relayed to me at that time, or maybe it wasn't known then, but his ability to secure the final permits for this monumental development would ultimately have a tremendous impact on the future of our project.

Again, let me stop here and interject a thought: in the midst of our workaday lives, we just don't stop and smell the roses often enough, and this was one of those days for me. I had become so wrapped up in selling the project that I didn't savor the moment. Of course, at that particular time, I really didn't really know the people involved — we were all strangers to each other. All I knew about Mr. Tanaka was what was relayed to me by Mr. Conyngham, and all I knew about Mr. Conyngham was what he was willing to share with me about himself. As my relationship with Mr. Conyngham has continued over the last 19 years, he has only, with some insistence from me, shared a bit of his background and his life in a most humble way (and these thoughts are expressed now only with his permission.)

When I learned how many different languages he could speak, I had to ask, "How in the world did you ever learn to speak so many different languages?" The short answer was that he traveled a lot. He went on to say that, after World War I, his father was appointed as British ambassador to Japan and China. Though he was merely a boy, as they traveled by boat on long voyages across the Pacific, his father insisted that he learn to speak those languages.

At that time, very few Europeans could speak the Japanese language, which put him in a critical position as an interpreter and negotiator. Some of his unique experiences included working with the World Bank, teaching economics at the University of Tokyo, serving as a member of the Olympic Committee, and hosting the likes of Bobby Kennedy and Frank Sinatra. When I first met Mr. Conyngham, he had just resigned his position with the Ritz Carlton organization. During his tenure there, he was successful in arranging financing between international partners to develop Ritz Carltons around the world. He also assisted in selecting strategic, exotic locations for expanding the Ritz Carlton chain worldwide.

That was an eventful day, because, once again, all our future hopes of North Augusta's riverfront becoming a reality rested on the outcome of that initial meeting. We had done all we knew to do and really all we could afford to do. As we returned to our cars, Mr. Conyngham relayed to me that Mr. Tanaka was interested in learning more about the project and would like for us to arrange a meeting with the Port Royal Group to see where things could go from there. We could see they were excited about the project; it was difficult for them to contain themselves. No words were spoken about making a deal—just arrange a meeting.

I called Ron and relayed the events of the day— that the Japanese had expressed an interest in learning more about the project and asked for a meeting to view a presentation and meet all the players. Several weeks later, after Mr. Tanaka's first visit, the stage was set and the players were there: John, Zack, Mr. Conyngham, Nobu, Mr. Tanaka and his entourage; the Port Royal Group and their attorneys, and me. This would be another red-letter day. It was show time at the Apollo, and although John and I had done many presentations in the past, we had never stood before such a prestigious audience.

The meeting was held at the office of the Port Royal attorneys in an impressive oak-paneled conference room designed to intimidate. I asked myself, "What the heck am I doing here?" Nevertheless, this is the moment John and I had prayed for, and this was no time to flinch.

The meeting started at 9 a.m. and ended sometime after lunch. I led the presentation and tried to keep it low-key and light, but it quickly became a formal event — each word spoken had to be translated by Mr. Conyngham, and I'm sure that translating Southern English into the King's English was a challenge. By the end of the presentation, I believe we did an honest job of presenting all the nuances of the project while emphasizing the difficulties in acquiring the remaining 19 land parcels.

It is easy for me to remember the exact day of that meeting because it was the 30th of December, 1990... the day before New Year's Eve. It's easy to recall, because I received a phone call that night around 11:00 from Mr. Conyngham saying they wanted to become my partner in the project. I immediately called and woke John, gave him the news, and followed with a call to Ron, Port Royal's CEO. By the time I hung up, it was New Year's Eve and time to celebrate.

Although we were all excited about the prospects of having a new partner with the funds necessary to keep the project moving forward, I still had issues with Ron's demands that the Port Royal Group receive a larger percentage of the project than we thought they deserved. Nevertheless, the only option that John and I had was to play the hand we were dealt—keep our mouths shut and our ears open.

Mr. Conyngham asked that John and I and the Port Royal Group prepare a written proposal outlining the terms of a future partnership agreement. He went on to mention two items that Mr. Tanaka wanted included in the agreement that were crucial to his involvement. They were straightforward, simple and non-negotiable: first, Mr. Tanaka would be given the right to sell 150 international memberships to the Club and second, Mr. Tanaka would be given the exclusive right to name the golf course. Subject to those two conditions being met, Mr. Tanaka would agree to fund the entire project, which was estimated at that time to be around $12.5 million.

At this point things started to get more interesting: the Japanese were on one side, with Port Royal on the other —and John and I caught in the middle. Unbeknownst to me at that moment, this was a very enviable position to be in. That being said, Port Royal wanted the sole task of putting a proposal together with their attorneys. As you can imagine, their interests and underlying motives took priority over any of our concerns. What we thought was reasonable and in the best interest of the project and North Augusta's best outcome were totally ignored.

Port Royal's main focus at that time was to sell condominiums. That is certainly understandable, particularly when you have so much at stake. We were sympathetic to those issues, but that doesn't wash when the terms and conditions they asked of us and the Japanese were so one-sided in their favor. Port Royal wanted to retain a controlling interest in the project, a management fee stiff enough to choke a goat, and all that without investing another dime. In essence what they were asking for was the moon and the kitchen sink to go with it.

After reading their proposal, I remember telling Ron that what was being asked of Mr. Tanaka was ridiculous and that there was no way he would agree to such a one sided deal—and indeed he didn't. As a matter of fact, it was taken as an insult. I remember Mr. Conyngham commenting that he wasn't surprised, since the French and the Japanese have never worked well together.

I had to ask myself, "Why in the world would Port Royal come up with such an outrageous list of conditions that would cause the Japanese to walk away from the deal?" One possibility was that maybe they didn't want the Japanese involved in the project in the first place.

At that time the Port Royal group had a good working relationship with a French bank that was funding their condominium project. Maybe they saw the bank as a future player in our project, which they mistook as leverage in making such ridiculous demands for Mr. Tanaka's involvement. Whatever their reasons, they shot themselves in the foot. Mr. Tanaka wanted nothing else to do with the Port Royal Group. He saw it as a great project, but refused to go forward with the French. That put John and me back at square one, having to wait and see if Port Royal could interest their bank in funding the project.

By this time, their condominium construction was starting to experience some cost overruns, which meant that the likelihood of the bank participating in another project was nil. All the while, Mr. Conyngham was continuing to move forward with his plans for the bed and breakfast inn and still believed the golf course would complement his plans, regardless of who was involved. On one unexpected occasion, Mr. Conyngham called and asked if there was a buy/sell provision in our partnership with the Port Royal Group, to which I replied there was. Port Royal's attorney had drawn up the agreement and had included the buy/sell provision probably as boiler plate stuff that's normally included in a typical partnership agreement. You can be sure when John and I signed that agreement, neither of us expected the day would ever come when we would exercise that provision.

The way that provision was written, either party had the right to buy out the other party for the sum of $250,000 and then each party countering back and forth in $50,000 increments with the highest bidder being the winner. $250,000 was a lot of money in 1990, and for some of us, it is still a lot of money. Mr. Conyngham went on to say that Mr. Tanaka had expressed the desire to move forward with the project so long as the Port Royal group was not involved; and he would provide the necessary funds to make that happen, subject to the terms of his original proposal. For John and me, that was a no-brainer in light of Port Royal's "put that in your pipe and smoke it" demand. We were now in a position to let them smoke it — and smoke it they did.

A couple of weeks later John and I received a loan of $250,000 from Mr. Tanaka pretty much on a handshake and a one-page proposal saying we would work in good faith to structure a future partnership agreement subject to Port Royal accepting our offer to buy them out.

At that particular time, as Port Royal continued to feel the pinch of cost overruns, they seemed to have lost interest in what was happening on the South Carolina side of the River. The timing was right, and from the reports in the newspaper, Port Royal didn't seem to be in a strong enough position to continue funding the outstanding due diligence items as well as the earnest money deposit necessary to keep the project moving forward. If my memory serves me right, Port Royal was probably into our deal to the tune of $150,000 - $175,000 and, by my way of thinking, would likely welcome the opportunity to simply get their original investment back. I expressed that to Mr. Conyngham, and he assured me that Mr. Tanaka was not interested in stealing the project or giving the perception that the terms of our agreement were not being honored. That reassurance of my original assessment of Mr. Conyngham proved that he was indeed a man of integrity and principle. It was a refreshing change from so many other real estate dealings.

All our hopes now rested in Port Royal's response, which gave them the opportunity to make a counter offer of $300,000. I recall going by Zack's office and picking up a check in the amount of $250,000, immediately calling Ron to let him know I had a business matter to discuss with him.

It was a rather short meeting with only the two of us present. I vividly remember his facial expression: it was a total shock, having taken him completely by surprise; but I also sensed his relief and disbelief that this was happening. I have never liked the term, "business is business" and still don't. But to this day I believe the decisions the Port Royal Group made and the greedy actions they took precipitated that event and should have never happened. In hindsight, and knowing how much money and time was spent in assembling the outstanding land parcels, I believe Port Royal made a wise decision to accept our offer to buy them out. Over the course of their involvement, which was less than a year, they ended up making a tidy little return on their investment of around 80%. Needless to say, John and I were pleased the way things worked out—I think it was the best thing that could have happened for both parties. Nevertheless, having some new blood in the game boosted our confidence that we were now in a position to get the project back on track. I don't know exactly what Port Royal's agenda was when they got involved with John and me on the project, but I have to admit that without their initial help, it is doubtful that North Augusta's riverfront would have ever gotten off the ground.

Now that Mr. Tanaka was our new partner, I was confident that we had the financial backing necessary to complete the project. With Mr. Tanaka on board, we were also introduced to his team of U. S. lawyers who worked in Atlanta. As you would expect, they were one of the south's top law firms and, like our lawyer Zack, didn't mince words. They got right down to business, which works for me because I'm not much on small talk—let's just get it done.

Mr. Tanaka's lead lawyer was a young lady by the name of Melissa Hart. She was pleasant enough, but all business. On our first meeting with Ms. Fink in Atlanta, she made it plain to John and me that Mr. Tanaka was much too generous and she believed our contribution didn't justify our request for 25% interest in the total project. Of course we disagreed, and it was a moot point anyway because Mr. Tanaka had agreed to those terms prior to Port Royal's exit and was documented in a loan agreement that he had already signed.

Over the course of the next year, all during the due diligence and land acquisition phase, I spoke to Melissa almost daily. She never passed out compliments or congratulated us on achieving any milestone, but on one occasion later in the project, after she realized how much effort and work was involved, I was taken back by her comment. She said, "I don't believe 25% is enough—you guys deserve a larger interest." That was a nice thought but also moot. A deal is a deal: we thought it was fair then, and I still believe it was a good deal for both parties. Zack, our attorney for the next several months, worked diligently with Melissa to do the necessary research, tracing land titles and undoing the remnants of a tangled web of right-of-ways, easements and discrepancies in boundaries left by the original town of Hamburg.

It was a mess. In one particular instance, where we wanted to close an abandoned easement, court action was necessary which resulted in an unfavorable ruling by the judge giving an absentee landowner the leverage he needed to demand a ridiculous price for his property, which we eventually had to purchase. I have to say that no one likes to pay attorney fees, but Zack earned every dime, and he did it the hard way. We were fortunate to have someone with Zack's experience on our side of the table.

For the next several months we continued working with Mr. Tanaka, pretty much on a handshake, while Melissa was preparing the partnership agreement; it seemed that process was taking a lot longer than necessary. Also, it was still unclear that we would be successful in obtaining all the outparcels necessary to even say we had a project. I must admit, I still had some reservations that we would be successful in that regard. What John and I were delivering to the partnership was a positive market study, wetland approvals, HEC II modeling showing no rise impacts on floods from the river, and the Knox and Parks land purchase agreements. That was significant, but I knew what was in front of us—the difficulty of obtaining the remaining twenty tracts of land. While working with Port Royal, I had already plowed much of that ground and knew the success of the project rested squarely on my shoulders. I had met or communicated with most all the landowners on a one-to-one basis, even the infamous Mrs. Cochran, and had assessed their needs and hot buttons. The only landowner remaining to be contacted was Dr. Milton, who I later learned was a blood relative to Mrs. Cochran. I knew what I was in for, and I wasn't disappointed.

Dr. Milton's property was about thirty acres, with a northern boundary running parallel to the abandoned railroad right-of-way owned by Hamburg Industries. (This property now comprises today's 18th green, club-house and driving range.) I was told that the parcel had been originally obtained by a king's grant and had never changed hands. In other words, Dr. Milton had a religious connection to the property which would explain why he had no interest in selling this piece of antiquity, his family jewel. To compound the problem, Dr. Milton retired from practicing medicine years earlier, now living as a recluse with minimum contact to the outside world.

I followed my typical procedure in trying to contact Dr. Milton for several months, sending letters and calling his home to no avail. It was a dead end street, and I knew this couldn't go on forever—I had to find another way to get his attention.

I heard through the grapevine that Dr. Milton had a son who lived on the other side of the river in Augusta. My thought was to approach his son and have him plead my case, or at least get me an audience with his dad. I contacted him by phone and found him to be a most cordial young man. He was the complete opposite of his father, and most willing to meet with me. I remember him saying that he also had difficulty contacting his dad, but would try. He was somewhat sympathetic to my dilemma but offered no assurance that he could convince his father that the future of North Augusta's riverfront development was in his hands. That wasn't just a ploy to get his father to sell—it was the undiluted truth, a vital piece of a convoluted puzzle.

Several weeks later I finally got the call I had been waiting on: Dr. Milton's son informed me that his initial thought was correct—his father wasn't interested in selling and liked North Augusta's riverfront just the way it was—garbage dump and all. Once again my hopes were dashed, and I was back to square one, a place I was becoming all too accustomed to. Of course, Ms. Fink and Zack were informed, and when I broke the bad news to them I could hear the disappointment in their voices.

No one had a clue as to where to go from here. I was stumped. What do you do when someone doesn't want to sell their property and no amount of money will get them to move? I must admit I never anticipated anything like this. I had hit a brick wall and somehow I had to find the resolve not to give up. I guess that's when I started hearing all the voices from my past saying "where there's a will, there's a way;" "quitters never win." You know the clichés sound so good, but you finally begin to question their validity. As far back as I can remember, I've always believed most of us can do most anything if we set our minds to it, but this was different. I had no control over the situation and realized nothing short of a miracle would change Dr. Milton's mind.

If I was looking for a miracle, I found it in a very different strategy: somehow, Dr. Milton would need to realize that it was in his best interest to sell. If money wasn't a motivating factor, there must be something in his life that was important to him other than the thirty acres I was seeking.

In my search for that hidden truth, I found a curious piece of North Augusta's history. On the north side of the thirty acre tract was another piece of land owned by Dr. Milton that obviously held fond memories for him and, I surmised, his family as well. I never set a foot on the property because it was completely fenced with "Posted-Keep Out" signs lining its perimeter. I became aware of this parcel's existence from some old North Augusta history books and my subsequent visual inspection through a dilapidated vine-covered fence that ran parallel to the abandoned right-of-way owned by Hamburg Industries.

What I could see through the fence was startling and somewhat eerie. It was like looking at a sepia-tone snapshot that had been frozen in time some 50-60 years earlier. From my vantage point, I could see a spring-filled pond once used as a swimming hole with evidence of a sandy beach, a makeshift slide, a rope swing, and a rusted tin roofed wooden building that was obviously used for changing rooms. It looked as though someone had just walked out, closed the gate, turned the key—and for some unknown reason, left and never looked back. It was amazing how well the remnants of that once vibrant landmark had been preserved.

Discovering what was important to Dr. Milton was only the first part of the puzzle. What to do with that information and how to make it work for me remained the big question. In my quest to gain a better understanding of what made the Doc tick, I discovered he was also a car buff. I made an unannounced visit to his house located on Martintown Road across from Al's Auto Parts. Situated only a few yards off the road, the house was completely overgrown by vegetation, making it difficult to find my way to the entrance.

I didn't like the idea of walking up to someone's door unannounced, especially with them having no idea of the reason for my visit. Though I had been successful in personally contacting most all the other river property landowners, Dr. Milton, like Mrs. Cochran, was not your typical landowner. Anyway, there I was knocking on the

My first view of this old swimming hole near our property was like stepping back in time, given its remarkable state of preservation.

door with no response. I could see a car parked in the driveway and was sure the Doc was at home; so I continued knocking harder and louder. Still no answer. I thought to myself, "Maybe the Doc is hard of hearing," so I wandered around to the back of the house to the back door, again knocking loudly. It didn't take me long to realize this was a futile effort. Indeed the Doc exhibited all the characteristics of a classic recluse, but I'm not sure even an earthquake could have gotten him to the door. Frustrated, I walked across the street to return to my car, noticing several old cars parked on the side of the house. It was sort of like looking at a used car lot, but like everything else around there, they were all covered in vines, left there to rust to death. I continued walking, fearful it would now be impossible to acquire this parcel. Throwing in the towel wasn't my style, but if I couldn't get the man to talk to me, how in the world could I ever make him an offer?

Every time I hit a road block on this project God had given me the inspiration to keep going. Somehow a door would swing open or a different opportunity would present itself. This time, God put a person in my path named Al LaFavor of Al's Auto Parts, directly across the street from Dr. Milton's house. I had made Al's acquaintance years earlier when he was working as a city inspector for the City of North Augusta. He had since left the City and started his own business as an auto parts dealer. As I was returning to my car, I decided to go inside and thank Al for the use of his parking lot.

What resulted from that casual contact was an intervention similar to the one Mrs. Baynham had with Mrs. Cochran—only this time, it would be Al communicating my concerns to Dr. Milton. Out of all the people in our community, you would think there would be more than one person who had some type of relationship with Dr. Milton; but Al was the only one I knew who turned out to have something in common with Dr. Milton. That vital something was their passion for old cars.

As a previous city employee, Al was aware of all the scuttlebutt that surrounded our project, and he inquired of our progress. I told him, just as I had confessed to Mrs. Baynham a couple of months earlier:"not great," explaining the difficulty I was having trying to make contact with Dr. Milton.

Al immediately volunteered to help, if he could. He went on to say that the Doc would come over every so often and they would talk cars and, if the opportunity came up, he would try to encourage the Doc to at least meet with me. I expressed my thanks to Al and told him I would get back with him as soon as I had something in hand that I thought would get the Doc's attention other than money. All I had to do now was find that "something."

As a necessary part of my due diligence efforts, I had drawn up a composite map showing every piece of property either occupied by the golf course or contiguous to it.

Included was pertinent information such as owner's name and address, size and tax value along with some estimates of what I considered to be a reasonable offer. With that map and information in hand, I assigned priorities to each tract as it related to the golf course and surrounding land uses. Way down on my priority list, I discovered a small piece of property, maybe an acre or two, that was located on a high bluff overlooking the golf course property. It was a tract that wasn't crucial to implementing the golf course, but yielded great potential for some type of multi-family development once the golf course was in place. This property was also adjacent to Dr. Milton's property and overlooked a swimming hole that, for some unknown reason, meant so much to him.

In my desperation, it occurred to me that in lieu of offering just money, maybe a land swap or a combination of land and money might possibly be more appealing to him. My rationale centered on the belief that Doc would obviously not appreciate condos or apartments or some other type of high-density development intruding on his private memories. Flushing out that strategy would ultimately be the key to my success in acquiring his two acres.

My research showed the adjacent property was owned by an absentee owner living in Connecticut named Steve Curtis. It's interesting how easily I can remember his name, since I have never laid eyes on the man and only corresponded with him by mail or phone. The primary reason I can is because of the unique, unknown role he played in the development of North Augusta's riverfront. I'm sure he was unaware of it, but his willingness to trust me was truly miraculous — and that was the miracle I was looking for. Ultimately, he gave me the leverage needed to acquire the two most difficult pieces of property related to the project.

Anyway, I called Steve and introduced myself and expressed my interest in purchasing his two-acre tract without giving him much detail about the project, other than the fact I was in the process of trying to develop a golf course. To my surprise, he was amenable to selling subject to the purchase price being determined by a legitimate appraisal. I agreed and several weeks later we closed on the property without a hitch.

Over the course of corresponding back and forth with Steve, we developed a cordial friendship, and on one occasion he mentioned that somehow he was related to Mrs. Cochran and Dr. Milton. That was hard to believe, because I found Steve to be such an amiable person, so unlike his distant relatives. Somewhere down the family tree (and to his great credit) the gene pool must have improved. That would become even more evident several months later when I had to call Steve again for a major favor. More on that later.

Acquiring the property from Steve was easy. Now the real work would center on getting an audience with the Doc.

I knew the only way that connection would happen was with Al providing the liaison between us. Of course, Al was willing, so I took him up on his offer. All I really remember is writing and delivering a sealed proposal to Al which he personally put in the Doc's hands. The terms of the proposal included having the property appraised to determine the fair market value, with the Doc having the right to choose the appraiser. We would pick up the tab and include the Curtisproperty as a caveat. It was a straightforward deal. Al mentioned to the Doc that our intentions were to develop the adjacent property into some type of high-density development which was the truth, but in reality the possibility of that ever happening would not occur in his lifetime, or maybe never.

Days and weeks passed without a word from Al. My anxiety level was ramping up, knowing the clock was ticking on the Knox contract—this couldn't go on forever. I had made Al aware of how crucial the Milton property was to the success of North Augusta's riverfront, but I was also aware that Al had a business to run and, in the scheme of things, my problems weren't a major concern of his. At least that was my thinking, but just when I thought this great strategy of mine was about to come to another dead end, Al called with some encouraging news. He told me that the Doc just dropped by, was given my proposal and was willing to meet with me. I couldn't believe my ears. I thanked Al, but reflecting back on it, his willingness to help in this situation was one of the unsung stories that gets lost between the pages. This seemingly insignificant act, a friend simply helping another friend, became another essential step in the project's ultimate success.

Shortly thereafter, I recall meeting with Dr. Milton, standing in his living room discussing my proposal. It went off actually as scripted — terms, price and conditions all smooth as silk. That's ironic knowing how difficult it was to be standing there. The mystique that surrounded the Doc was there, all right: he was quiet and obviously not very well organized. Amongst the clutter, I noticed a stack of unopened mail and, to my surprise, there on top were my letters—unopened, unread, and obviously of no importance to him. It gave validity to my strategy and gave me a small sense of satisfaction that all this effort was necessary so that somewhere down the line it just might pay off. My next encounter with Dr. Milton was at Zack's office on the day we closed on the property. I recall the event as monumental, but for the life of me, I can't recall a single physical attribute of the Doc other than his conspicuous absence of conversation.

It's interesting to note during this critical stage in the project's development, when funds were necessary to complete transactions—whether it was earnest money owed, purchases or fees—Mr. Tanaka provided those funds without reservation and without a written agreement being in place. I seem to recall that close to $1 million was spent on a handshake while the balance of our due diligence items was still underway. The money was wired from Japan to the Atlanta attorneys; they would in turn wire the money to Zack, and he would disburse the money as necessary to complete land transactions, pay fees and other miscellaneous expenses.

We followed that procedure for several months. Negotiations with remaining landowners continued in hopes of tying up other critical pieces of property. Some acquisitions required very little cash; others demanded large earnest money deposits; others demanded an immediate closing. This put a great deal of financial stress on Mr. Tanaka, and the money began slowing to a trickle. To complicate matters even more, the Augusta Chronicle thought it newsworthy to visit the Aiken County Courthouse to research land closings that had been recorded and share that information with the general public. Of course that's public information and available to anyone including the landowners if they take the initiative to visit the courthouse and seek out that information for themselves.

What the Chronicle succeeded in doing, and I think it was intentional, was drive up the per acre price we had to pay for the properties we had not yet closed on. It also triggered a rash of landowners reneging on purchase agreements that had been successfully contracted. And those still in negotiations demanded more money for their property. Right or wrong, you may call this journalism at its best, but I saw this as an attempt to sabotage our project and keep North Augusta's riverfront potential from being realized. It seemed history was repeating itself, and the rivalry that had existed for more than one hundred years was still alive and well.

Once we closed on Dr. Milton's property, I felt fairly confident that we were over the hump and well on our way to achieving what others had not been able to do; or maybe they were just unwilling to pay the price. The land was expensive, but I consider it cheap compared to what it was costing my marriage and my family.

I was completely absorbed in seeing this thing through. Every day was spent trying to negotiate land contracts, corresponding with Mr. Tanaka in an effort to keep the money flowing, and dealing with the complexities of the due diligence and legal issues. Of course, when the sun went down and the lights went out in North Augusta, the other side of the world was just getting up. Many a night was spent waiting for the phone to ring, or for the fax machine to start ticking. If that weren't enough, my brain wouldn't turn off. My dream, which had only been a lovely possibility months before, was actually becoming reality. My mind's eye began to focus the vision with spectacular clarity.

When this project was conceived, the vision that Mr. Tanaka and I shared was never a residential golf course community. Having houses lined up like little soldiers on the banks of the Savannah River was the last thing we wanted to see happen to this strategically-placed piece of property. Even before Mr. Tanaka became involved with the project, the concept I shared with Mr. Knox was comprised of an elegant, upscale public golf course. At the time we contracted with Mr. Knox to purchase the property, the land was a designated FEMA flood plain, which greatly complicated any potential residential development. It certainly could be done, but the finished floor elevation of any house would have to be one foot above the hundred-year flood elevation, meaning houses would have to be constructed on pilings set ten feet off the ground. We were well aware of these limitations from the start, which made the golf course concept extremely viable, since it was a permitted use in a flood plain.

I recall my very first meeting with Mr. Knox during which he mentioned the prospects of the hundred year flood elevation being reduced. I was aware of that fact and it was local knowledge that Georgia's former Governor, Carl Sanders, owned a large amount of property just south of our tract. He was in the throes of doing battle with the Corps of Engineers to lower the hundred year flood elevation. Knowing it would literally take an act of Congress to get that done and fully aware of how that battle had dragged on for years, I really didn't believe he would be successful in that endeavor. I'd be willing to bet Mr. Knox agreed with my assessment and it may have ultimately influenced his decision to take a chance on selling us the 170 acres.

So the golf course concept and its feasibility was never predicated on whether or not the Governor would be victorious. What drove the concept from the beginning was simply this: could a great public golf course be successful in that location?

Of course, hindsight clearly shows that I underestimated the Governor's tenacity. The evidence is obvious considering all the residential development that has subsequently taken place on the banks of the Savannah River. This added revenue has swelled the coffers of the City of North Augusta and lined the developer's pocket; but the original golf course concept would have protected the riv-

The International Club course was refined to be a truly great golf course with eighteen memorable, environmentally-sensitive holes — a concept that Mr. Tanaka and I absolutely agreed on.

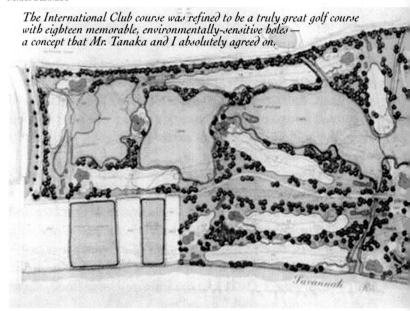

erbank from visual intrusion by preserving existing trees and vegetation along the river's edge.

A lesson I learned while working with the golf course architect George Cobb, along with my personal experience playing the game, is that truly great courses have great finishing holes that create an unforgettable impression lingering in memory long after the round is over. The banks of the Savannah River were reserved for that purpose in the initial design.

The ninth hole, a par four playing up-river from the east, would spell disaster for a player who hits an unintentional hook: the Savannah would claim its prey. The eighteenth hole, I believe, would have been called "the Jewel on the Savannah," designed to make or break a round. Unlike the ninth hole, this reachable par five hole played down-river with the sun at your back. A slice or a pushed shot would prove perilous and loom heavy in the golfer's psyche knowing what was out in front of him. Playing a

heroic second shot over the lagoon that would set directly in front of the green would assume a two-putt. A player would then be assured of an easy birdie and possibly an eagle. Both the ninth and eighteenth holes would return to a clubhouse perched above a presentation green with docks directly below. It was designed so that a shuttle boat would routinely ferry visitors and players back and forth across the river to share the amenities both sides offered. Yes, the creation of a great golf course with eighteen memorable holes was the vision Mr. Tanaka and I shared. If ever real estate was involved, it would only be to complement the total golfing experience.

At this point in the project's history, we were about eighteen months into the contract with Mr. Knox with only six months left to closing. Daylight was burning, and I knew Mr. Knox well enough to know this was business and his payday was only six months away.

When Mr. Tanaka became involved in the project,

the only background information John and I were given about him was that he was a successful golf course entrepreneur in Japan who owned several courses there. His current Japanese golf project, which involved pushing a mountain into the ocean was being executed while the necessary permits were still in process. Mr. Conyngham remarked to me that Mr. Tanaka had already invested $38 million into the project and still had not received his permits. Whether or not he ever obtained those permits, I don't know—but the flow of money to our little $12.5 million project slowed to a trickle. As the cash flow continued to deteriorate and money pressures mounted, there were many sleepless nights spent waiting for the phone to ring, eagerly anticipating some good news. It seemed like weeks and sometimes months between those calls.

When we actually got to speak to someone on the other side of the world, little or no encouragement was offered, only an ambiguous promise that the money was on the way—but when? Getting any firm commitment remained elusive. Of course, I would hang on those words with no alternative but to believe they were true; all the while the clock continued ticking. I was beginning to see the handwriting on the wall, and it was becoming alarmingly clear that we were not going to meet the closing date. According to the terms of the contract, Mr. Knox would become the beneficiary of all our due diligence work. I couldn't let that happen.

Anticipating a worst-case scenario, I began conversations with Mr. Knox, pleading my case for extending the contract closing date. I called and he agreed to meet with me at his office in Thomson, GA. It was eerily similar to same situation I found myself in some 22 months earlier, me sitting there like a schoolboy with hat in hand. All the while, Mr. Knox maintained his usual stoic composure, waiting for me to break the ice with the first word.

The author, Mr. Nakamura and his associate, and John Thomas.

I was hoping Mr. Knox would find it in his heart to be gracious and maybe sympathetic knowing all John and I had weathered over the last several months. I believe Mr. Knox was generous, but his generosity would cost us $50,000 for a sixty-day extension. He didn't have to do that, and I don't believe he would have if he had simply been interested in regaining control of the property.

Nevertheless, the pressure was on, and we had to come up with $50,000 in a hurry. I called Melissa, Mr. Tanaka's attorney, and faxed Mr. Conyngham, asking for his assistance. A week before our drop-dead date, we received $50,000. I hand-delivered it to Mr. Knox in Thomson; he signed the extension and we dodged a bullet for another sixty days. Based on what I was told, I assured Mr. Knox we'd be ready to close in sixty days. That wasn't the way it turned out. Eventually there was a closing, but I would have to make two more trips back to Thomson, humbly pleading my case. Each time the price went up and the extensions got shorter. During those extension periods, our personal money pressures mounted. Just how long we could continue to hold on was doubtful.

Little did we know that our project was about to enter into its most bizarre phase. About the time the last extension was due to expire, I received word from the Japanese attorneys in Atlanta that Mr. Tanaka was coming to the U.S. to bring some potential investors to view the project. John and I took that as good news. That was all the information we were given, other than that one of the individuals had a car dealership in Japan specializing in classic automobiles.

We wanted to get off the dime and were growing weary—just holding the project together had become extremely difficult, so we were more than ready for some encouragement.

A couple of weeks later Mr. Tanaka and his entourage arrived in Atlanta and were chauffeured to North Augusta in a white stretch limousine. The major players in this party were Mr. Tanaka, Melissa Hart (attorney), a Japanese interpreter and a potential investor by the name of Nakamura and his personal entourage.

After so many years, two significant moments of that particular visit remain etched in my mind. The first was when the entire encourage arrived at the site and we made our way to our previously cleared observation area looking back across the river to Augusta. For a few minutes, the tone of the conversation was pretty normal and cordial— "normal" of course meaning that we couldn't understand a single word other than an occasional "hi," meaning yes. Then abruptly, the tone and the intensity of the meeting changed. It wasn't at all clear what was going on. It was only several months later that we learned exactly what had transpired there.

I mentioned the white limousine only because of the

events that took place on the drive back to Atlanta. I wasn't in the car, but the way the story was relayed to me was that Mr. Tanaka was "made an offer he couldn't refuse." I was only told this after Ms. Fink had resigned from representing Mr. Tanaka and was no longer involved in the project. I don't know if it would have changed the outcome of the project if we had known the truth earlier, and she was certainly under no obligation to tell us anything. I think she knew much more, but the lawyer/client confidentiality clause precluded her from saying too much. What she did say was that intense negotiations between Mr. Tanaka and Mr. Nakamura continued on the drive back to Atlanta and that the Japanese interpreter was translating the conversation so she could understand everyone's position. The negotiations and the tone of the conversation intensified to a point when Mr. Nakamura commanded the interpreter to stop translating, causing the interpreter to turn pale with shock. Melissa said the animated conversation continued, culminating in total silence as Mr. Tanaka was left with no alternative other than to agree.

Later that afternoon I received a call from Melissa, who indicated that John and I needed to be in her office first thing the following morning. She gave no clue why — just be there. We were left completely in the dark as to the significance of the meeting.

Having no idea of what had transpired in the limousine, we were completely caught off guard as Melissa introduced Mr. Nakamura as our new partner and majority owner of the project. In short, Mr. Nakamura had acquired Mr. Tanaka's position — lock, stock and barrel. Mr. Nakamura was now in complete control of the project. Needless to say, John and I were shocked at the news, but Melissa was quick to add that nothing had changed concerning our position as 25% limited partners and project managers. During that entire meeting, I don't believe Mr. Tanaka said a single word. After a year or so of working with Mr. Tanaka, I had come to regard him as more than a business partner—he was a real friend. He shared my vision; as a developer, he knew the difficulties in launching a new project. That meeting was a very solemn occasion. It would be the last time I ever saw or spoke to Mr. Tanaka.

His true sensitivity had become apparent to me after spending all day with him at the Master's tournament. That evening, several of Mr. Tanaka's associates and I were having dinner at a local restaurant when, in the background, "I Left My Heart in San Francisco" began to play softly. One of his associates told me that Mr. Tanaka's wife had died while they were visiting San Francisco and that she was buried there. I could tell that Mr. Tanaka's demeanor had suddenly changed. It was obvious that he had truly left his heart in San Francisco.

Another gentleman, and I use that word loosely, was introduced to us in Melissa's office as Kalani Chow. Kalani was a dark-skinned Hawaiian, dressed in the customary native garb of flashy flowery shirt, khaki pants and Dockers. We were told that Kalani was a trusted associate of Mr. Nakamura's and would function as the chief financial officer for the project, a position that the Atlanta attorneys had heretofore occupied. In other words, when the money left Japan, it was wired to Kalani, who would be responsible for seeing that the money made its way to Augusta. It did—well, at least a portion of it did.

Several months later after the money started flowing again, Mr. Nakamura's attorney in Japan, who only spoke broken English, called Zack and asked for an accounting of the money he had received from Kalani. Zack referred him to Bobby Oswald, the project's accountant. Somehow, things weren't adding up: on this side of the pond, none of us knew actually what that meant, because we were never told specifically how many millions Kalani had received. I'm sure the language barrier didn't help, but in my way of thinking, Kalani was a most improbable candidate to be in such a trusted position. Nevertheless, it wasn't my decision. Mr. Nakamura was the general partner, and Kalani was his man. I understood that the Japanese way of doing business was not the same as ours; but the most puzzling thing to me was how relaxed they were about spending money and how nonchalantly they treated this project.

To make my point, I had invested years in putting this project together, and then one day a guy with questionable development experience tells me that money is no object and that we are to buy every piece of property we can get our hands on. Whether these guys could be trusted or not was simply irrelevant to the situation we were in. They were in control and the ball we had been pushing uphill for over a couple of years was now on a downhill slide. I couldn't stop it, but determined I was to not let someone else screw the project up, even if they had all the money in the world. I was determined to see this through, come hell or high water.

I never really got to know much about Kalani, and I don't mean to judge him too harshly. The only thing he ever told me about himself was that he owned a strip club on one of the Hawaiian Islands, and I know he enjoyed gambling. On his excursions between Augusta and Hawaii, he would frequently make a stop in Las Vegas. I'm guessing that those stopovers may account for some of the missing funds that never made their way to Augusta.

Now that we had money in the bank and a mandate to purchase all the property that surrounded the golf course and beyond, we starting closing on individual parcels as quickly as possible. We were given a new lease on life; now we had to run with the ball to make it happen.

To my recollection, this was when things really got fun. Up until now, when negotiating with land owners, my goal was to arrive at a price at or below the appraised value. Now I was being told, "Just buy it and don't worry so much about the price." That attitude didn't make good sense to me and never influenced my approach in negotiating purchase prices with the landowners. The only exception, however, was my final negotiation with the infamous Mrs. Cochran.

This shrewd old lady who had only months earlier in front of her pastor said she would be fair-minded in negotiating a fair purchase price subject to my acquiring all the other properties first, would now be tested—tested as to how her definition of fair-minded lined up with reality.

To my way of thinking, an appraisal performed by a reputable appraiser of her choosing would be the fairest way to determine the property's fair market value. That wasn't to be the case.

The day arrived. We had persevered and successfully obtained contracts on all the surrounding properties and already closed on several parcels. I had met the one condition Mrs. Cochran required and contacted her by phone explaining my desire to complete our negotiations on her 14 acres on the river. To my surprise, and in her cross, harsh manner, she informed me that she didn't know anything about real estate transactions and that it would be necessary for me to contact her son-in-law who was a real estate agent in Columbia, SC. She provided me with his name and phone number and made it clear that all negotiations would go through him. When I heard those words, I knew this wasn't going to be good, but it was the only alternative I was given.

My previous suspicions of Mrs. Cochran were just beginning to be manifested. My gut instincts were about to be confirmed in glorious detail: I couldn't trust this lady. She had me over a barrel. I knew it — she knew it — and I was sure her real estate son-in-law knew it too!

I called her son-in-law, introduced myself and scheduled to meet him later that afternoon in the lobby of the Sheraton Hotel at exit #64 on I-20 in Columbia. On the hour's drive up to Columbia, all sorts of thoughts were running through my head. This guy was in real estate and surely he would know the value of wetlands and flood plain property, but would he be fair-minded — or had he and Mrs. Cochran conspired to cook my goose?

This guy (I don't recall his name) had described himself to me so that I could recognize him; but I had no problem spotting him as he came strolling across the lobby, primarily from the grin on his face. He looked like the cat who just ate the canary, or was about to. I'm sure we exchanged some pleasantries, but I was anxious to hear the fair-minded number that he and Mrs. Cochran had formulated, so I wasted no time in asking the question. "How much?" He wasted no time in answering the question. "Four-hundred fifty-thousand dollars" came rolling off his tongue! Those words just flowed out so easily.

I'm sure I must have looked like a deer in headlights. I was dumbfounded, speechless. I couldn't believe what I was hearing, and what made it even worse was that he was grinning ear to ear during the entire conversation. "Take it or leave it" was his response when I asked how he could justify those numbers as being fair-minded. I remember him saying, "I know you need those 14 acres or your project is dead." He was right about that: Mrs. Cochran was playing me like a fiddle, and I regretted being so kind, trusting her to be fair-minded in placing a value on her land. What she and her son-in-law were asking for her property was 8-10 times higher than what the per acre price was on adjacent properties.

I took it as a personal slap in the face from these people who cared little about killing the project and North Augusta's hopes of ever developing its riverfront. I left that short meeting red-faced and steaming all the way back to North Augusta because I was determined I couldn't let this happen. I had to find some type of leverage to get Mrs. Cochran to be reasonable.

In telling the outcome of this situation, I do so with some reluctance—because it didn't change the dollar values so much as it created within me a desire for getting even. I wanted Mrs. Cochran to squirm and feel the loss of something she really valued.

There's a saying that all's fair in love and war, and I considered this war. My love for the river property drove me to find a way to humble these two characters. They needed a dose of reality when it came to placing a value on the property, or something close to it.

After much pondering, the only idea I thought might work was to find another piece of land and work out yet another land swap, as I had done with Dr. Milton. The parcel that came to mind was a tract adjacent to her home on Butler Avenue.

What was unique about this tract was that it contained a small family cemetery. An old wrought-iron fence surrounded the weathered headstones that lay in the front corner of the property. I recalled Mrs. Cochran alluding somewhere in one of our earlier meetings that this was where she would be buried. But when I researched the courthouse records, I noticed that Mrs. Cochran didn't own that parcel—it was actually owned by one of her distant cousins, who went by the name Steve Curtis. If you remember, Steve was the landowner I never met who sold me the property on the bluff overlooking the river. Ultimately, that purchase provided me the leverage I needed to get Dr. Milton to sell. I hoped it would work the same for Mrs. Cochran.

In all the transactions that took place in putting the river property together, this had to be for me the most challenging and rewarding. It was a most unusual request that I was about to propose to Steve, and a strange one at that—one I had thought about for some time before I approached him with the idea. Steve didn't know me, but what I was about to propose to him involved a matter of absolute trust.

When I called Steve at his home in Connecticut, he remembered me from our previous transaction regarding the purchase of his property overlooking the river some months earlier. I shared with Steve the difficulty I was having in acquiring Mrs. Cochran's 14 acres and asked if he would sell me his lot adjacent to her home on Butler Avenue. Steve stated he wasn't interested in selling and went on to say that if he did sell, he would incur the wrath of God if he didn't sell it to Mrs. Cochran. I explained that I had no interest in doing anything with the property other than using it for leverage in getting Mrs. Cochran and her son-in-law back to reality. I pleaded my case and explained the significance her 14 acres held for North Augusta's future in its effort to develop the riverfront.

Somewhere during the conversation with Steve, he stated that he was well aware of what I was up against. He told me a story about being at a graveside funeral with Mrs. Cochran when she spit on a grave, and said that she probably had a screw or two loose. But even knowing that, he didn't want to create any more rift in the family and was reluctant to sell me the property for fear of the repercussions. It was at that point I got personal with Steve and asked that he just trust me. I don't know about you, but when someone asks me to trust them, a red flag goes up. That's a difficult thing to do. I don't like asking someone to trust me, particularly someone I've never met face to face. What a ridiculous request to make! Nevertheless, I made it with a gentlemen's agreement and handshake over the phone, so to speak: regardless of what happened with my project or its impact on the future of North Augusta and the riverfront, I would see to it that Mrs. Cochran ended up owning that parcel of land. Also, Steve agreed that if Mrs. Cochran contacted him, he would not disclose the details of our conversation.

With that unwritten agreement in place, I went to work. I told Steve I would have the property appraised and draw up a purchase contract in that amount, but would not close on the property until I had an agreement with Mrs. Cochran. He agreed, subject to those verbal conditions. A couple of weeks later I had a signed contract in hand and was ready to do battle. I wasn't sure how all this was going to turn out, but knew I had something that Mrs. Cochran wanted. I knew she would hate to see someone other than herself controlling her future burial plot.

What I did next was mean-spirited. It was my way of getting even with Mrs. Cochran for playing me for a fool. I must say with so much riding on the outcome, revenge was sweet.

At the time I had no problem justifying my course of action. I called my surveyor, Tripp McKie, and told him I had a piece of property that was going to close and that I needed to have the property surveyed. Without divulging any details, I asked that he start early the next morning and put a large crew on the job. My next request must have sounded a bit bizarre. I wanted him and his crew to make as much noise possible as they cleared the property lines — I'm sure he wondered what the heck was going on!

The next morning, that picture assuredly became crystal clear when Mrs. Cochran came running out of her house raising Cain and threatening to call the police if he didn't stop. All the while this was going on, I was sitting patiently by the phone waiting for the fireworks to start, and start they did. As expected, Mrs. Cochran called me saying I had better get up there and stop what was going on. My plan was working better than I had imagined. Payday was here, and I was enjoying every moment.

Anyway, when I drove up I could see the pandemonium I had created with this little charade. I politely asked Mrs. Cochran to settle down, as she continued ranting, so I could explain my intentions. I explained to her that she was not honoring her word and her promise to be fair minded in selling me the 14 acres. I also let her know that she had, in essence, single-handedly killed my hopes of developing North Augusta's riverfront. She didn't agree or disagree. All she said was, "You get in your car and go to Columbia right now and work this out with my son-in-law!" I agreed to do that only on the condition that the two of them return to reality, to give me a price that was sane, a price that was in keeping with her word that she would be reasonable in placing a value on the property.

I know the Bible tells us to love our enemies. I viewed Mrs. Cochran and her son-in-law as greedy people, threatening my vision of what North Augusta's riverfront could be. I had set my course and couldn't let their greed kill my dream. Never in my wildest imagination would I have thought I would be encountering this many difficulties, or that I would have to resort to these shenanigans to bring a dream to life.

As Mrs. Cochran requested, or demanded, I immediately got in my car and drove to Columbia in hopes of putting this matter to bed. To this day, every time I drive past the Sheraton on I-20 in Columbia, I remember the conversation I had with Mrs. Cochran's son-in-law. We hadn't even made it to the lobby when he made the comment, "I know what you are trying to do," implying that it wasn't going to work. Standing there in the parking lot, with my face ablaze, I said, "You don't get it; you have killed my project. You've made sure of that with your greedy demands!" The frustration was beginning to mount as I told him, "I drove up here at Mrs. Cochran's request, and if I'm wasting my time, you can explain to Mrs. Cochran that we can't work it out."

He further insulted my intelligence with the following proposal: they would pay me 10% more for the Curtis property if I would agree to sell, offering no concession to reduce their original asking price of $450K on the 14 acres. I know I'm not the sharpest tack in the box, but the more he talked, the redder my face became.

Finally, I couldn't take it anymore and told him that wasn't going to happen. In a rather nasty tone I told him, "Hell will freeze over before Mrs. Cochran gets her hands on that piece of property. I will put it in my will that the property will never be sold and will always be owned by a Bennett from now to eternity." My rant continued by saying, "I plan to build a modest rental house on the property."

At that point, I think he was starting to get my drift. The canary-eating grin that betrayed his persona wasn't quite as wide as it had been moments earlier, and the conversation began to take on a more reasonable tone.

To make a long story short, we did eventually arrive at a number that, in my opinion, was still too high. But the lawyers in Atlanta told me that my new Japanese partner was okay with the price and to make the deal. I know we could have negotiated a much lower number now that we were in the driver's seat, but I was also aware of the promise I had made with Mr. Curtis that regardless of what happened, Mrs. Cochran would eventually be the beneficiary of his property. So we made the deal and closed on the 14 acres which included the parcel on Butler Avenue. At the risk of sounding anticlimactic, what we achieved with that acquisition was the ability to complete the routing of all the holes as originally conceived.

That highly sought-after piece of property is now occupied by holes number 16 and 17, which were two of my favorites. Hole #16 was originally designed as a driveable par 4, and #17 a short par 3 requiring an accurate shot over a massive area of wetlands. In the earlier construction stages, as these holes were being cleared, I wanted to determine the difficulty of these holes, which would be influenced by the strategic placing of the tee boxes. This was a memorable moment for me. After all the hullabaloo we had been through, it was certainly worth the effort.

It was a bright, sunny morning as Don McMillan, Steve the "dozer" operator, and some other workers watched my golfing prowess, which amounts to long off the tee and short on the greens. Putting has never been my strong suit, but I was confident that this little par 4 had the making of a great golf hole if, indeed, it wasn't too easy. Before my gallery of onlookers, I proceeded to tee it up, and then I teed it up again… and again. The strategy of this hole called for a heroic shot off the tee and eventually I did manage to get my Sunday punch across, giving credence to the fact that with persistence, it can be done.

It was absolutely thrilling to see my vision physically coming to life: trees being cleared and dirt being moved, knowing that we now had the financial backing in place to complete the project. However, believe it or not, of all the memories etched in my mind, the one that jumps out most clearly is the day I handed Mr. Knox the million dollar check.

As previously mentioned, the original two-year closing had lapsed. That was the two year closing date Mr. Knox described as "unheard of." It had come and gone, and his willingness to grant several extensions proved that he had made a good decision. He had granted those extensions based on my word that our Japanese investors would come through with the cash. If he had said no to those extensions, I honestly believe that all the success of North Augusta's riverfront we have now witnessed would not be here today.

North Augusta's future really was held in the importance of that closing day, but that's not what I was thinking of. In my mind I was seeing the three of us — Zack, Mr. Knox, and myself, sitting in Zack's conference room, signing the closing documents. As I passed Mr. Knox his check, he surprised me by giving me a check in return: it was my original $100.00 earnest money deposit that he had never cashed. Handing my personal check back to me, he commented, "Mark, I think you have earned this." I thought that was a cool thing to do and a bit out of character for Mr. Knox, but I did appreciate the sentiment.

You would think when receiving a million dollar check that showing a little emotion would be normal. As usual, though, Mr. Knox maintained his trademark stoic demeanor. As he was walking out, I remember thanking him for giving me this chance, even when he and I both knew this was the longest of long shots. He said something like, "I'm glad it worked out," and that was it.

Zack and I chatted for a couple of minutes longer,

when we heard wheels squealing and the sound of cars crashing. Dashing outside, we discovered Mr. Knox had pulled his black Lincoln out in front of another car and got smacked. It wasn't enough damage to report, but it gave me pause to wonder if Mr. Knox was a little more excited about receiving that check than he let on.

After we made sure everyone was okay, he returned to his car and drove off down Greene Street. Although that was the last time I saw Mr. Knox, my admiration for him still keeps his memory alive in my mind.

In all my dealings with Mr. Knox, he always kept his word. There wasn't any ambiguity—I knew exactly where he stood and could deal with that.

Thank you, Mr. Knox.

NEW LIFE, SHORT-LIVED

Now that we had acquired all the necessary land parcels to complete the course routing and had the required permits in hand, we could physically begin construction of the golf course. By this point, I had tweaked and refined the design of the golf course many a time. I found it hard to believe that my new partners wanted me to find a golf celebrity to give it a once-over and sign on as the designer of record.

To me this exercise was a waste of time and resources, and I didn't like the idea of someone else taking the credit for my creation. That's called pride, of course. But I'm of the opinion that if you can't take pride in what you're doing, or if you don't have a passion for it, you need to find something else to do.

I expressed this opinion to no avail and realized that Marshall Bennett would likely never be a household name in the golfing world. I also recognized the added value a big-name designer brings in marketing real estate, although real estate was not in the equation at this point in the project's history. I swallowed my pride. I was in no position to do otherwise, and all I wanted was to start moving dirt.

Where does one start to find a golfing celebrity that

wants to work with a no-name designer? That was the question I posed at that time to the late Phil Harrison, a member of the Augusta National and legendary starter of the Masters Tournament. Mr. Harrison was a celebrity in his own right and a consummate gentleman.

John and I met Mr. Harrison in the late seventies when we moved our fledgling design firm from North Augusta to Augusta. We rented a second-story office space from him in the Campbell Building on Eighth Street, which sat directly over Bubba Farr's Restaurant. It was a great space for growing our firm. I remember that when Mr. Harrison was showing us the office space for the first time, he rode us down on the elevator, packed with 50-pound bags of onions and potatoes. That elevator opened directly into Bubba Farr's restaurant. Mr. Harrison jokingly commented that not only were we getting a great office space, but our own personal elevator to the hottest lunch spot in Augusta!

We were in that space for only a couple of years and struggled to pay our rent on time. I recall that there were several occasions when we had to ask Mr. Harrison to extend us a grace period to come up with the rent. He was always gracious in that regard and rode it out with us during those early, lean years. Later, as our insurance needs grew, we reciprocated by having the Harrison Insurance Agency provide all of our insurance coverage and maintained that relationship throughout our business career in Augusta. Mr. Harrison's agency also provided all of our insurance coverage for the River project.

He was naturally the first person I thought of who would know an abundance of golf professionals. I went by his office, told him about my dilemma, and asked if he had any suggestions or recommendations as to who would be a candidate, with the necessary credentials and celebrity status to satisfy my new partners. He thought for a moment and started reeling off several names, some more popular than others. I say that carefully, because if one has the credentials to play in the Masters, one obviously has the golf credentials. However, two additional ingredients were essential: this man's name must be synonymous with golf, and he must be willing to put his reputation on the line working with someone he's never heard of.

As a friend, Mr. Harrison stuck his neck out a little, but I also think he recognized the making of a great golf course with some great holes kissing the banks of the Savannah River. He saw my vision and had no hesitation in picking up the phone and immediately calling Raymond Floyd.

I wasn't quite prepared for that and wasn't sure where this was going, but I thought to myself, "This is pretty cool." After the usual pleasantries, Mr. Harrison made my introduction and handed me the phone. Ray and I chatted about the project and established a little rapport, then scheduled a trip for me to fly to Miami to go over the project in more detail, to see where things would go from there. Ray did eventually become involved with the river-front project, which led to us working together on another golf course design outside Nashville, TN.

My Miami flight touched down on a Sunday afternoon. Ray and I had scheduled to meet the next morning around nine at his home on Indian Creek Island. I was aware that he was playing in the Doral Tournament that weekend, so I was eager to check into my hotel, then hustle over to the "Blue Monster" to see the conclusion of the tournament. Unfortunately I didn't make it, but did catch the news report later that evening that announced Ray's victory. I was elated and thrilled for him, but thought that all the fanfare around that victory would probably complicate our meeting the next morning.

I anticipated that things might be a little crazy around Ray's home for the next several days and was prepared to reschedule. Bright and early Monday morning I called Ray's home, and he answered the phone. I congratulated him on his victory and asked if it was still convenient to meet with him. He asked, "Where are you?" and quickly gave me directions to his home. We met for several hours, reviewed the plan, and talked golf philosophy and hole strategy. He liked what he saw, then gave me the contact information for his agent. Several weeks later, we completed our contractual agreement with Ray and welcomed his involvement with the project.

Finally, after three years of constant struggling and haggling, John and I could see a little light at the end of the tunnel. Our elusive partnership agreement was now in place, including the original terms as previously agreed to by Mr. Tanaka. Kalani was flying back and forth between Hawaii and Augusta with little involvement in the details of the project. He just needed to keep the money flowing. All the necessary approvals were in hand; Phase I construction contracts were signed; and the physical construction of the golf course was underway.

I would be remiss in telling this story if I didn't stop here and give credit where credit is due. As a designer and visionary, my work isn't complete until my creation is on the ground—and actually getting it on the ground is another story. That's where a gentleman named Don McMillan enters the picture. What you see on the River today was constructed by his skilled hands.

Prior to meeting Don, John and I had worked with a grading contractor out of Aiken, SC on several other non-related golf course projects, and we were considering hiring him to build the course. He had constructed several

Don McMillan, Raymond Floyd and the author looking over a course design.

courses in the Aiken area, and our previous track record
with him was solid.

I was in the process of reviewing his proposal when a
representative from Don's company found me on site and
asked if it was too late for Don's company to bid on the
project. Though I felt confident proceeding with our decision to work with someone we had previous experience
with, I felt it would be a good idea to have a comparison
bid, just to keep everyone honest. Several days later I met
Don McMillan. We spent the day on site, walking over
the property and discussing the scope of work involved in
constructing the course.

I knew immediately from Don's credentials and project
portfolio that his experience would be invaluable to the
ultimate success of our project. His credentials included
working with notable golf course architects such as my
former employer George Cobb as well as Tom Fazio,
Arnold Palmer, Jack Nicklaus, Joe Lee, Willard Byrd,
Robert Trent Jones and a host of others. Courses in
Don's repertoire included Shipyard Plantation, Wexford,

Indigo Run, Dataw Island, Windemeyer Country Club, Beauchen and others, totaling 150 courses or more. No doubt, Don's credentials were impressive, but the factor that I ultimately based my decision on had less to do with his experience. It had a great deal more to do with his personal integrity. Let me explain.

Prior to meeting with Don, I had done some investigation on my own and discovered Don's company was rebounding from bankruptcy, which is the kiss of death in trying to secure new work. I really liked Don but felt I couldn't afford to take a chance on someone who might jeopardize my investors or the project. I was torn with having to make the hard decision.

What tipped the balance in Don's favor was when he voluntarily disclosed his financial situation to me without reservation. He knew what was at stake and it could very well have cost him the job. He wanted to make sure I was aware of his situation at the start rather than disclosing it somewhere down the line. That was not only the right thing to do, but it was gutsy—and that's an attribute that's hard to find.

All of that took place some twenty years ago. The decision I made then was based on a man's integrity, and it has been one of the best decisions I've ever made. To this day, Don and I have completed more than a dozen projects together and have maintained a friendship highlighted with some great projects and war stories: truly an adventure that has been worth the ride.

With Don on board and the centerline of the holes staked, we broke ground with Mr. Nakamura, with myself hitting balls down the #1 fairway that Don had previously cleared for this auspicious occasion. That was the start of construction, and at long last my vision was coming to life.

The first order of business was to get rid of all the

garbage that had accumulated on the western end of the property primarily occupying holes #9, #10 and #16. Originally, we planned to transport this material off site, assuming there was hazardous material somewhere in the rubbish. Upon further investigation and several thousand dollars later, engineering studies determined that no hazardous materials were present and the most practical way to dispose of the debris was to bury it. Don had earlier suggested burial as an alternative to hauling the stuff off site, but we had assumed the worst case scenario, which was estimated at $350,000 to $380,000 for clean-up. Right off the bat, Don's experience and expertise in environmental studies had saved us a ton of money. The materials previously considered a liability were turned into an asset by providing needed fill material for building the mounds around the perimeter of the holes. Finding enough suitable fill material on site had always been a major concern — it had to be scrounged up from every conceivable source within the confines of the property.

The bulk of the fill material was generated from the existing lakes that dot the property, which proved to be an challenging operation since the site's existing water table was so high. Another issue that proved to be a constant problem was the number of bricks that kept rising to the surface. Years earlier, the property had been the site of a brick manufacturing plant, evidenced by some old kilns discovered on site. Culled brick, broken and unusable, had at one time been disposed of all over the property. These kept popping up during the final grading operations and had to be physically picked up and removed. This never-ending process caused Don to affectionately refer to this course as "the golf course from hell." From our perspective, it was a name that fit.

Just when things were starting to look up for John

Don broke ground for an official start to construction, and my vision was finally coming to life.

and me, a bolt of lightning struck out of nowhere. We never saw it coming, but come it did, and it turned our world upside down. As I recall, it started as a typical day—my sons getting off to school, my wife heading out the door to work, and me drinking my last cup of coffee before heading upstairs to my 8' x 10' home office. It must have been about 7:30 when I received a call from Zack, our attorney, asking if I had seen the morning newspaper. I told him no, and he suggested I get it immediately, read the front page article and call him back. I couldn't imagine what this was all about, but could tell from the urgency in Zack's voice that it wasn't going to be good. As I'm writing this, it seems like only yesterday, but after twenty years you would think I would have forgotten it by now.

There are days in all of our lives that we never forget — days that have such a devastating impact that they change the course of our lives. Unaware of it that morning, a lot of lives were about to change.

I ran down the stairs, out the front door, grabbed the newspaper, and before I could read a word, there in the middle of the front page was Mr. Nakamura's picture. As I sat there on the steps of our veranda, my heart started to pound as I discovered that my newly-acquired partner was allegedly involved with the Japanese underworld. The article went on to say that monies invested in our project were part of a money-laundering scheme, which could be the kiss of death for our project.

I immediately jumped in the car, getting to Zack's office in record time. He was as floored as I was and couldn't offer any comforting words that I so desperately wanted to hear. Zack had been involved with this project since its inception and had witnessed our highs and lows. This new revelation was the lowest of the lows. How we were to maneuver around this one, if we even could, was yet to be determined.

That momentous blow triggered others that seemed to keep us spiraling downward. Just when we were recovering from one blow, there would be another left hook right behind it. The next one occurred a week or so later when I walked out my front door and found my house surrounded by an onslaught of news reporters from Japan. It looked like a circus, with lights and cameras set up all over our yard and people running up shoving microphones in my face. I was overwhelmed, to say the least. Obviously, our little project on the Savannah River was big news in Japan, but more than that, I think it was the word "Augusta" that attracted great interest in the story.

Anyway, they were disappointed with what they got from me. I couldn't understand half of what they were saying and with legal implications pending, I thought it best to continue this interview in Zack's presence. I called Zack and asked if he could rescue me from these guys. He said, "Bring them over." I don't think Zack or his office staff realized what they were in for.

As you can imagine, it was a zoo: all those reporters, cameramen, lights and microphones all crammed into Zack's conference room. Under different circumstances, this could have been humorous but, rest assured, I wasn't laughing. Strange, I can't recall a single question from that interview. I knew it had aired in Japan after I received a call from one of Mr. Tanaka's associates telling me we were celebrities, and our project was big news there. It was obviously not the kind of publicity we were seeking for our golf course. This project was supposed to be about great golf holes gracing the banks of the Savannah River, not about gangsters.

Let me say here that I knew this wasn't just another bump in the road. It was an apocalyptic show-stopper. That became even more apparent when John and I received a call from the FBI and the U.S. Customs Department. For a couple of days, John and I were grilled with questions to which we had no answers. All we knew was that Mr. Nakamura owned and operated a classic car dealership in Japan and enjoyed playing golf. That's it. How he came to be our partner was by default. Our previous partner, Mr. Tanaka, owned 75% of the partnership which included the 1% general partnership interest, giving him complete control of the project. He then sold that interest to Mr. Nakamura and didn't have to ask our permission to do so.

You would have thought Mr. Tanaka's attorneys would have conducted some serious investigations prior to Mr. Nakamura's potential involvement. I desperately wanted to believe that Mr. Tanaka was duped, just as we were. The lawyers in Atlanta were employed by Mr. Tanaka and were looking out for his best interests, not necessarily those of John and me. It all goes back to "He who has the gold, rules."

The most devastating news that came out of those

meetings was answered when we asked the question, "How does this impact our project?" We were told that the most likely scenario would be that the U.S. government would seize the project, sell it, and return the proceeds to the Japanese authorities. They suggested we sell the project ourselves before the government got involved. That was a bitter pill to swallow and it didn't go down easily.

From the start, John and I believed in this project, and that all the sweat equity we had poured into it would ultimately be our retirement plan and take the financial pressures off our families. The golden ring that was just within our grasp was slipping away. Selling the project was the last thing we wanted to do. It would mean giving up on our dreams, bringing the sacrifices our families had endured over the last four years to naught. It would be admitting utter and complete defeat.

From that horrible day when Mr. Nakamura's picture showed up on the front page of the Augusta Chronicle, it was as though a dark cloud hovered over the project. Everything we tried to do was like pushing a string—it just doesn't work. It seemed as though the harder we pushed, the worse things got. Another nail in our coffin came when the mayor, city manager and city council, all of whom had enthusiastically supported the project in the past, bailed on us. Sure, that was the politically correct thing for them to do, but it hurt. I had served as a member of our local planning commission for eight years and had worked diligently to change the non-progressive image of North Augusta. In addition, I had worked shoulder to shoulder with the City Manager and planning staff in assisting to establish boundaries for a newly-conceived redevelopment district. These folks were old friends—we had shared lunches and partied together, and now they were running for cover. Trying to attract a new financial partner without the City being 100% behind the project would be impossible.

As I recall the events of those dark days, the realization was becoming more and more evident that my dreams, hopes, and aspirations of success in all its forms were being washed away. The old adage I had grown up with — where there's a will, there's a way — had deceived me. I saw myself as a failure and a victim of my own dreams. How could a project so noble and so right take me to a place of such despair? Finally, ultimate despair hit when my wife of twenty years said she couldn't take it anymore and wanted out. In all my years of living, I had never felt so alone and deserted, left with the illusion of what might have been.

It's difficult to write about this stuff, but the stuff dreams are made of isn't always pretty. I've heard it said the things that don't kill you only make you stronger. That may be, but it assumes you have the strength to get up and go after it again. I think it also assumes you spiral down about as low as you can go before you can get back up.

How do you know when you've hit rock bottom? That's a question I thought I would never have to ask myself. I've always viewed my life as an adventure, accepting and even relishing the highs and lows, always believing some good would come from a bad situation. In the midst of this dismal situation, knowing the devastating toll it was taking not just on my family but also on John's, I could see nothing good coming. My noble vision of saving the North Augusta riverfront had now become my nightmare. I wanted it to just go away. The cost was too great: the thought of sacrificing my family never entered into the equation.

I remember there was a lot of soul-searching during those dark days and most of it came in the still of the night. When sleep wouldn't come and praying didn't seem to help, I found solace in taking long walks. I remember many sleepless nights, putting on my tennis shoes, quietly slipping out of the house, and just walking. Eventually, I would be drawn down Lake Avenue, through town, leaning over the rail on the 13th Street Bridge. I stared angrily at a project that once was, asking if this is how it ends.

Thank God I wasn't a drinker or I wouldn't be here telling this story. My walk would continue across the bridge and up Broad Street, through the seedy end of Augusta with all of its neon lights spelling "SIN." Under normal circumstances I would never have ventured into that spot, for I would have feared for my life. On one of those occasions, I found myself hoping for someone to just hit me in the head and stop all the madness that encompassed my life. That was my darkest moment, but thankfully it passed. My pace quickened and I continued my way back across the 5th Street Bridge, up Martintown Road and, eventually, to the security of my own veranda.

Two remarkable events happened during those dark days that altered my thinking and ultimately, this story's outcome. Some reading this will view these events as coincidences, others as insignificant, and maybe some as answers to prayer. That's your choice.

The first one came on a hot summer evening shortly after supper when a stranger showed up at my front door. I opened the door and he introduced himself as a sand salesman. He went on to say he had heard about my plans for a golf course on the river and wanted me to purchase sand from his company. He dove into great detail when describing the different qualities, colors, and granular sizes of his sand. That was all very interesting, but we hadn't broken ground yet, so a sand discussion was a bit premature.

At that time of the evening, I wasn't interested in discussing sand qualities and tried every way possible to get this guy to go away without being too impolite. He didn't take the hint, and just kept talking. The more he talked, the more obvious my efforts became to get rid of him. Regardless, he was a good salesman, persistent to the point that he wanted me to physically stop what I was doing and take him to the river to show him where the course was to be built. I told him that was pointless, that there was nothing to see but trees. After a lengthy discussion, I finally realized I wasn't going to get him off my front porch until I agreed to show him the golf course location on the river. It didn't make much sense in the least, but I reluctantly agreed to show him. As we approached the narrow muddy entrance to the property, I noticed an abandoned white car stuck in the mud. I recall making the statement, "We have trespassers, and they have no business here." I safely parked my car on the last remaining piece of high ground to avoid getting stuck myself. The salesman and I were going to have to walk the rest of the way.

We had only gotten about 100 yards or so into the property when I saw a sight I'll never forget. There, in the middle of the road, sitting in a huge mud puddle, was a little old lady. While we were some distance away, I heard her shouting these words, "Thank God, He's answered my prayers!" As we approached, she continued proclaiming those words over and over, "Thank God, He's answered my prayers!" We walked up to her, not understanding what she was doing there. "Ma'am, you seem to have a problem," I remarked, which was a slight understatement. The sand salesman and I waded in the mud and, as gently as possible, secured the lady by her arms and got her to her feet. As you can imagine, she was covered with mud

Just a few yards away, an alligator had taken up residence in a small pond along with water moccasins and copperheads.

from head to toe and was quite embarrassed. My first reaction was to explain to this dear lady that she needed to let us take her immediately to the emergency room so she could get some medical attention. She wouldn't hear of it. Assuring us that she would be all right, she asked to be taken home.

She went on to explain that she had gotten up early that morning and drove to City Hall, a few blocks from her home, to pay her water bill. Unfortunately, on her way there she found the road had been blocked off due to a washout from a storm the day before. The detour caused her to look for a place to turn around and somehow she ended up getting her car stuck in the mud. From there she decided to get out of her car and start walking out. Only problem was, she started walking the wrong way. She had obviously slipped and fallen, and found herself sitting in that mud puddle all morning and most of the afternoon. It's amazing that she survived. Just a few yards away, an alligator had taken up residence in a small pond along with water moccasins and copperheads.

Now here's the reason for telling this story. While we were driving this little lady back to her home, she asked if we could do her a favor and drop her at her back door so her neighbors wouldn't see her covered in mud. That wasn't a problem, but the statement she made, I've never forgotten. She said in her soft, gentle voice, "Mr. Bennett, sometimes we need our prayers answered just to keep our faith built up."

I've thought about that a lot over the years and sometimes we do need evidence that God hears our prayers and that He also answers them. I know God heard her prayers, because I had no intention of going down to the site that day. I would have never gone had it not been for the sand salesman on my front porch, insisting I show him the location of the golf course. Another question I've often asked myself, "Who was that guy?" It's strange—I can remember his face and what he looked like, but I can't remember his name. I don't remember getting a business card from him, and I never heard from him again. Go figure. All I know is that God answered the little lady's prayers, and in a most miraculous way.

Of course, I've always believed that God hears our prayers. Witnessing how He intervened in her moment of need gave me pause to think as I stared down into the dark waters of the Savannah River. A voice in my head kept saying, "Mark, there's much beauty in this world left to be seen. You don't want to miss it." During those dark days, as my world and marriage were crumbling around me, I didn't know where to turn. Saving the project was no longer the major struggle in my life. Now I was scrambling to save my marriage and my family. Not having the ones I love in my life—losing them felt unthinkable.

I knew I needed answers from someone I could trust. There's a verse in James that says, "the prayers of a righteous man availeth much," and on this particular occasion I saw the car of a righteous man parked right across the street, in my neighbor's driveway. I recognized the car and knew that my previous pastor, Dr. Charles Page, had stopped by for a visit with Mrs. Baynham. Charles was now pastoring a church in Charlotte but would often stop in at Mrs. Baynham's when in town. At the risk of embarrassing myself, I ventured across the street and asked Charles to pray for me and my family.

I realize that not everyone reading this believes in the power of prayer, but I have firsthand knowledge that proves otherwise. I don't know whether it was my stubborn human nature or not, but to humble myself, swallow my pride, and ask for God's help was my last remaining hope. I was in a desperate situation and knew I needed divine help. So I prayed—and I'm forever grateful that God heard and answered those prayers. That's the only explanation I can give for why our marriage survived. It defies human logic. Based on the circumstances at that time, it's only by God's grace and His presence during the difficult years that followed, that my wife and I had the courage to keep looking for and find the love we once had for each other.

Looking back twenty years later, I can testify that God is still hearing and answering prayers. The words of that little lady stuck in the mud still ring as true for me today as they did then: "Sometimes we need our prayers answered just to keep our faith built up."

Now that the FBI and U.S. Customs had confirmed that our financial partner was indeed funneling money into the United States through illegal means, everything came to an abrupt standstill. Since Mr. Nakamura controlled the 1% general partnership interest, John and I did not have the ability to seek funding from other sources. We had nothing to offer, and nothing to sell.

The only correspondence or connection over the next

several months to Japan was through Mr. Nakamura's attorney, who only spoke broken English. It was Zack's recommendation that we seek to acquire the 1% general partnership Mr. Nakamura controlled. It was the only possible solution to win back the project and keep it moving. This endeavor went on for several months, and Zack's frustration level was soaring to new heights. This became painfully evident on many occasions as he tried to communicate with Mr. Nakamura's attorney by phone, urging him to relinquish the 1% general partnership interest or we would be forced to seek a legal remedy.

While this bickering was going on back and forth across the Pacific, I received a letter from the Corps of Engineers that informed me our mitigation work was behind schedule. I have discovered over the years that government agencies could care less about financial concerns, profitability, or even aesthetics. For them, it's all about rules, regulations and enforcement. Nonetheless, they were right—we were behind schedule and we had agreed in writing that $750,000 would be allocated to the restoration of those wetlands surrounding the project.

The Corps of Engineers gave us two options—one, to implement the mitigation plan per our original agreement; or two, remove the impacts and restore the property to its original condition, which would cost millions and be virtually impossible. But there was also a third option—do nothing, which would mean threat of financial fines and legal implications. Once again, John and I lay between the rock and proverbial hard place. The only difference this time was that the rock was more like a boulder. The only way we could move it was with Zack's help.

If matters could have gotten any worse, we had no source of income during these awkward days. Zack was working around the clock to make sense out of this chaotic mess. Forgetting the fact that the monies Mr. Nakamura had contributed to the project had been allegedly acquired through illegal means, his attorney argued that the money belonged to Mr. Nakamura, who wanted his money back. Our argument, which wasn't much of an argument at all, was that regardless of where the money came from or how it was acquired, it was gone, spent primarily on land acquisitions and paying for outside consultants. Furthermore, all the money that had been spent and as to how and when the funds were released came directly from Kalani Lau, Mr. Nakamura's hand-picked associate in Hawaii. During the course of the project, John and I never received funds directly from Japan or Kalani. They were always wired personally by Mr. Nakamura or his associates to Kalani, from Kalani to Atlanta, then to Zack. The only time John and I saw those funds was in the form of checks paid out to individual landowners at the closing table. Consultant fees over a certain amount were paid in the same manner, directly from the attorneys. John and I were also treated as consultants and received payment for services rendered.

Eventually Zack was successful in convincing Mr. Nakamura's attorney that the project was dead in the water, and that the only hope of getting any of his money back was to transfer the 1% general partnership interest to John and me thereby enabling us to sell the project. This would then enable us to pay off the vendors and implement the mitigation plan. Another strong determinate for relinquishing the 1% interest was the threat of an impending lawsuit fought out in a courtroom, which I'm sure would have been covered by the media on both sides of the Pacific. Under that scenario, a lot of questions would have been asked, not only about the source of funds, but also more unwelcome attention would have been focused on Mr. Nakamura and his associates. In hindsight, that probably would have proven to be a worthier long-term outcome for John and me.

Regardless of Mr. Nakamura's motives, papers were eventually signed, giving us controlling interest of the project. We certainly thought at that point we had dodged another bullet, given the amount of equity that had been dumped into the project ($5.5 million). Finding a new financial partner seemed like it would be an easy chore, but what we discovered was just the opposite. Mr. Nakamura's 74% limited partnership interest proved to be an anvil around our necks and his alleged ties to the Japanese mafia certainly didn't help our cause.

With the Corps of Engineers still breathing down our necks, it became imperative that we immediately find funding to implement the mitigation plan and stave off another legal battle. This would also give us the time needed to seek another financial partner to replace Mr. Nakamura, thereby clearing another hurdle and making the project more attractive to potential investors. Of course, Zack knew our situation and suggested we call Mr. Boone Knox with Allied Bank, who might be willing to loan us the $750,000 needed to implement the plan. Boone was the logical choice of lenders since his father, Peter Knox, was the landowner who gambled with us in the beginning.

We met with Boone at his office in Thomson, Georgia. I had never met the man before and he seemed cordial enough, but he absolutely shared one of his father's attribute—all business. You would think that with a $5.5 million asset pledged as collateral, you would certainly have ample equity to secure a $750,000 loan. It wasn't enough. In order to obtain the loan, John and I had to sign personal guarantees. Those guarantees weighed heavily on our minds over the next two years as we endeavored to save the project, or sell it.

With the loan in place, we immediately went to work implementing the mitigation plan and were successful in getting the Corps of Engineers off our back. At the same time, we began seeking other potential investors, preferably to assume Mr. Nakamura's position or, as a matter of last recourse, to purchase the project outright. When we began this process, we anticipated success in attracting a new financial partner, all the while retaining our original 25% interest. This seemed to be a reasonable request from our perspective, particularly since we would be delivering the project on a silver platter, so to speak. We had jumped through all the hoops, assembled all the land parcels, had all necessary permits in hand, disposed of the garbage on site, and at this point, we still had the City's support with a commitment to fund a portion of the infrastructure. We also had the 1% general partnership interest which we then discovered was a double-edged sword. We controlled the fate of the project but we also had a fiduciary responsibility to our 74% limited partner, regardless of who he was or his alleged connection to the Japanese mafia.

Kalani was history—we lost all communication with him. The legal implications of Mr. Nakamura's fate in Japan was unknown to us. Despite this, over the next several months Zach still received the occasional phone call from Mr. Nakamura's attorney wanting to know when his client was getting his money back. All Zach could say was, "They are working on it."

From our original inception of this project, I had been possessed by a driving force, knowing that with God's help I could do this. But now, with my marriage in shambles and the project teetering on disaster, I was beginning to question everything, and asked myself, "Where is God when I need Him?" The can-do attitude and enthusiasm that had propelled me to keep pushing had disintegrated. An occasional article in the Augusta Chronicle publicizing our beleaguered project and notorious Japanese partner kept the wounds open, reminding me and everyone else on both sides of the river that we had failed.

Both John and I were unwilling to accept failure as a possibility and lived in a state of denial for the next year or so. The hunt continued as we tried to find a new financial partner to replace Mr. Nakamura.

Those were extremely difficult days. We quickly learned after talking to a couple of investor groups that there was no conceivable way Mr. Nakamura was going to get 100% of his investment back, particularly in light of his cavalier approach to land purchases. Once Mr. Nakamura booted Mr. Tanaka out of the partnership, we were told by Kalani to purchase all the property surrounding the golf course, even those parcels not necessary, to complete the routing of the holes without haggling too much over price—just buy it. That cavalier strategy may work well when taking the long view in developing surrounding properties, but our potential American investors took the short view. They were looking for an immediate return on their investment.

Over the course of this dismal time, John and I met with at least a dozen different investor groups. We first offered to sell the project to the City of North Augusta, which would have given them complete control over North Augusta's riverfront. They demurred and elected to take a "let's see what happens" attitude. Personally, I think they made a mistake. In the early planning stages, even prior to Port Royal's involvement, protecting the river's edge from potential development intrusion was a major concern. The only structure that was ever slated to be visible from the Augusta side of the river was the clubhouse. Also planned was a presentation green with a central dock that would function to ferry patrons back and forth across the river, fostering mutual benefits for both the Georgia and South Carolina sides of the river. Preserving and protecting vegetation along the river's edge would have provided pleasing views looking back across the river from Augusta, thus protecting Augusta's back yard. This enhancement would also have served the total golfing experience by creating two of the most challenging and visually aesthetic holes in the CSRA.

In our quest to find a new financial partner, we thought the most logical place to start, after being rejected by the City, would be to approach local investors and developers. We had worked with several in the past and knew they had the financial capability to take on and complete a project of this stature. What we discovered, however, in almost every instance was a lot of interest, but it took weeks and sometimes months to determine how genuine their interest levels really were.

I remember working for months with a local group that I knew quite well. John and I made our initial presentation, explaining the project's history and its physical limitations, which at that time were minimal. As mentioned earlier, former Governor Carl Sanders had taken on the U.S. Government and was successful in arguing that the two major dams upriver prevented potential flooding along the river's edge downstream. Once FEMA's flood elevations were changed, the flood plain property we had acquired at an exorbitant price, averaging $12,100-$18,000/acre, skyrocketed in value. When we originally acquired it, the property had limited development potential. Now considered high ground, it had virtually unlimited development opportunities. Even in the early '90s, riverfront property with development potential was selling in excess of $100,000/acre. In other words, our 270-acre project had jumped five times in raw land value! Knowing that fact, John and I remained optimistic that even with all the negative baggage of the project's history, we would eventually be successful in finding a financial partner willing to assume Nakamura's position.

We were contractually obligated by the terms of our settlement agreement with Mr. Nakamura to make every possible effort to return all or at least a portion of the capital he had invested. That's what we intended on doing, but we soon discovered potential investors took note of the precarious position we were in, with a $750,000 loan we had personally guaranteed. A one-year due date on that loan made it impossible to negotiate favorable terms for either Nakamura or ourselves.

As that due date continued to close in on us, it felt like a noose around our necks. With every passing day, potential investors stopped calling and the noose got a little tighter. They hovered around like vultures just waiting to pick our bones. Needless to say, those months were some of the worst of my life. I've heard it said that "action is character," that "it's not what we say, but what we do that determines who we are." Finding the courage to take action—to suck it up and keep moving—was becoming increasingly difficult.

There was a lot of crazy stuff going on. The mitigation work on the wetlands was being completed, yet the reality was starting to set in that we may not be successful in finding a new financial partner—nobody willing to purchase the project, lock, stock and barrel, who would take it all, including the bank loan and the pressure that came with it. No doubt about it, we were in a desperate situation.

It was about this time that I received a call offering only a momentary glimmer of hope. An associate of the former Governor of Georgia called and indicated that the former Governor was aware of our project and asked if I would be willing to personally meet with him in Atlanta to go over the details of the project. "Of course," was my reply. I was acutely aware that the Governor's interest was based on the fact that he and his development partners owned several hundred acres downstream, and they had battled for years with the U.S. Government so that his land could be developed without the costly restrictions that applied to developing in the flood plain.

He won his battle, and our little 270-acre project also benefited from the reversal of those restrictions. But as previously mentioned, our initial goal was simply to build a quality, successful golf course that the public would enjoy playing. That was our original intent, but the precarious position John and I were now in forced us to consider most any offer that made sense.

The meeting with former Governor Sanders was set. I was asked to come alone, so the following morning I followed my instructions and made the drive over to Atlanta in record time. I carry with me some vivid recollections of that day. First and foremost was the meeting place. You've got to remember I'm the kid from Nellieville. I can't remember the name of the building, but was told I would have no problem finding it; just take I-75 North and look for a skyscraper that has been capped off with a mass of scrap iron that forms some type of modern art. They were right—I recognized the building immediately and managed to maneuver my way around Atlanta, honing in on that beacon of iron perched high above the maze of asphalt and concrete below.

Once inside this marble fortress, I took the elevator per instructions to the designated floor. As I stepped out of the elevator, I was taken aback by what I saw. It wasn't quite what I expected, not that I had given it much thought, but these surroundings were foreign to me. I wasn't prepared to step into a museum, but there I was surrounded by finely hewn marble structures of the Governor's head looking back at me. It seemed that every corner of the foyer had a bust of the Governor's likeness. I immediately concluded that the man I was about to meet didn't have a self-image problem. On the contrary, he must have a pretty healthy ego. Rightly so, he was a good governor and served the State of Georgia with distinction.

After being completely intimidated by my surroundings, the Governor and I met and discussed some of the details as to why I was there. He was well informed, knew that we were seeking a financial partner to assume Mr. Nakamura's position, and that we weren't in a very strong negotiating position. He went on to explain how he had been successful in taking on the U.S. Government, fighting for years to get FEMA to change the 100-year flood elevation on the river. He then divulged in a rather straightforward manner his own plan for developing North Augusta's riverfront.

I was well aware of his residential development downstream from our site and how sales there had lagged for years. People on the coast are accustomed to building 10 feet off the ground, but buyers in our area saw this as an additional expense and had a hard time buying houses set on stilts. Of course, with the subsequent flood elevation change, that area was now high ground and houses could be constructed using traditional building methods.

The Governor's plan, as he explained it, seemed to make some sense in that he wanted me to reroute the golf course so that nine holes would be relocated down river, onto his property. On the surface that seemed like a reasonable request, but the Fifth Street Bridge separated these two sites with a 35-foot high embankment, stretching about 75 yards across, covered with concrete and asphalt. I saw that as a physical obstacle that would be virtually impossible to overcome. Besides, at that point in time, all the fairways had been cleared, the wetland impacts were in place and the mitigation plan was being implemented. His request was posed as yet another, "take it or leave it." I was told, "If you can't make it work my way, I'm not interested." I guess we could have tunneled through the embankment costing millions more and years wasted trying to get approvals. Maybe there was some creative solution I hadn't yet given thought to, but certainly not one that would eliminate the mounting pressure we were under. The Governor's request, even if it was remotely feasible, would be like starting over. The prospect of putting my family and my marriage through several more years of grueling agony had no appeal to me. It would be much too difficult and I didn't have the stomach for it Although this occurred some twenty years ago, I recall that the Governor's response to my lack of enthusiasm to his plan seemed to set him back a little. I guess he thought it was worth a try, but I just didn't share his vision. It had no appeal to me.

The best alternative would have been for the Governor to purchase our project outright. However, I surmised he was aware of our precarious position and would rather pay a dime on the dollar instead of buying Nakamura out.

At that point in time, we were still trying to get someone to purchase Nakamura's 74% equity position, even at a fraction of its value. I assume the Governor, like other investors we had approached, would wait us out and buy the project at a foreclosure sale. On my drive back to Augusta, I was disheartened but not surprised by the turn of events and chalked it up as another wild goose chase.

It was now blatantly obvious to me that the worst case scenario was at hand. After countless ill-fated attempts to sell the project or even find a new financial partner, I knew my time was running short. It was just a matter of weeks before Boone and his bank would come calling.

It was on my drive back to North Augusta that I verbally asked God to take over. I don't know what took me so long to do it. Maybe it was my ego, not wanting to let go of my dream. Or maybe I feared being perceived as a failure. Those thoughts sure enough crossed my mind, but I think the truth is, I knew I had gotten myself into this mess and was man enough to ask God to help me get out of it. That being said, it was hard to ask God to take over, to let go of my pride. Yet, I distinctly remember in that moment turning the situation over to God.

I said, "Lord, I don't know how all this will turn out. I might lose it all—my marriage, family, house, friends, and the project. It's all too much, too complicated—too convoluted. I've tried everything I know to do. It's not working. I give it all to You."

At that moment the weight of the world was taken off my shoulders. The peace of God filled my spirit, my confidence revived. Proverbs 3:5 says, "Trust in the Lord with all your heart and lean not unto your own understanding; in all your ways acknowledge Him, and He will direct your paths."

We've all heard that God takes care of fools and children. I realize it's only by God's Grace that I have survived some of the foolish and stupid things I've done in my life. Case in point: several weeks after my meeting with the Governor, I received a call from Mr. Nakamura's attorney. He informed me that Mr. Nakamura was in Augusta and that he wanted to meet with me as soon as possible. I thought his passport had been pulled by the authorities in Japan while he was still under investigation for his alleged involvement with money laundering, so I didn't understand how he could possibly be here. Without thinking or hesitating or telling anyone where I was going, I immediately jumped in my car and drove to the Sheraton Hotel on Bobby Jones Expressway. I remember fuming as I hurried down that short interstate drive, still angry that he had sabotaged our project and destroyed my vision of developing North Augusta's riverfront. I think my anger clouded my judgment. I forgot who I was dealing with.

When I got to the hotel, there was Mr. Nakamura in the lobby, surrounded by several associates. I was greeted by his attorney, the same attorney with whom Zack had successfully negotiated to acquire Mr. Nakamura's 1% general partnership interest. He spoke only broken English but I caught his drift pretty quickly: Mr. Nakamura was demanding his money back, but I already knew that. So why was it necessary to fly 7,000 miles to tell me that in person, in a meeting that lasted only 15 minutes?

I think the message he wanted to convey was one of intimidation. I got it. Unlike some of the meetings in the past when pleasantries preceded the discussion, there would be none of that this time around. No hand shaking, no bowing, no sitting down, nothing. His attorney did most of the talking, or should I say yelling. He commanded that his client get his $5 million back. I warily explained why that wasn't going to happen, particularly with all the negative publicity surrounding Mr. Nakamura. At one point during those vocal assaults, after Mr. Nakamura saw his attorney was getting nowhere, he himself became livid. In an attempt to get his attorney to be more direct, he lashed out, emphasizing the importance of a safe return to his money. Again, I got the message, but I still question whether or not he got mine.

I told his attorney, rather emphatically, the simple truth. I had lost it all—my family and wife of 25 years, lost respect in the community, lost friends who somehow thought I might be involved with this sordid affair, and lost the project I had dreamed about and given my all to for eight long years. At that moment in time, I really didn't care about anything, let alone his dirty money. I felt like my life was over and Mr. Nakamura could do whatever he damn well pleased. There was nothing he could do or say to me that would alter or remove the black cloud hanging over the project, and my life. This was all of Mr. Nakamura's making, and I resented the fact that John and I were implicated in something we had nothing to do with.

That was my last encounter with Mr. Nakamura.

Have you ever questioned why things work out the way they do? My grandmother would quote Romans 8:28, "All things work together for good to those who love God, to those who are called according to His purpose." Over the last twenty years, I've questioned where the good lays in all of this. The golf course is there. North Augusta's vision of developing its riverfront has been realized and the community continues to grow and flourish. No doubt, good things have happened, but for me the greatest good comes in telling how God answered my humble prayer in a most miraculous way.

By this time in the project's history, there were only a couple weeks left before the banks started foreclosure proceedings. Our investor groups had already milked us for all the nuances of the project and knew they would most likely be in a position to purchase, at or below the original amount, the Corps of Engineers' mitigation plan, which John and I had personally guaranteed. The loan was originally $750K and had ballooned to well over $1 million due to accrued interest and loan extensions, not to mention the $5 million plus which Mr. Nakamura had invested.

John and I had already prepared ourselves. We were keenly aware that we would be forced into personal bankruptcy in order to cover any shortfalls between the loan amount and the foreclosure sales price. The final countdown had begun. We were both tired of fighting and anxious to get back to a normal life.

Then something strange happened that cannot be explained.

The timing of a family death is an event that only God controls. My wife's aunt had died suddenly, and we made plans to attend the funeral. After the service, all the family members gathered at the aunt's house to enjoy some Southern cooking and to reminisce about all the good times we had shared. To escape the crowd, I retreated to the veranda and was asked by one of the cousins how things were going in North Augusta. I remember meeting him on only one other occasion and was aware that he was a hotel developer in Atlanta. I reluctantly shared my dismal situation, never expecting anything to become of it other than making conversation to pass the time and escape the pandemonium going on inside the house. We talked for awhile. Before leaving he mentioned that he knew some folks in Atlanta who might be interested in taking a look at the golf course project. I took that as a polite gesture, one that I had heard numerous times before. I catalogued that conversation in that overcrowded category and dismissed it as small talk. Besides, we were on such a short fuse (only a week or so to go before the bank was to take over) that there was no possible way to do in a week what we had been unsuccessful in doing in two years.

In my mind, it was over. I was prepared for the worst. I considered myself a victim, not consumed by greed. In truth, I had been captured by a vision and it had consumed me. Now the aftermath of that vision was becoming mind-numbing reality.

The following Monday we were back home in North Augusta when I received a call from a man in Greensboro, Georgia. I had no clue who he was, but he went on to explain that Brenda's cousin had told him about our project and he was anxious to see the plans and any other information he could share with his associates in Atlanta. You would think I would be excited about the prospects of another group being interested in looking at the project, but I had already had this same conversation too many times. I couldn't take any more and wasn't interested. It sounded exactly like every other wild goose chase, especially when this guy I didn't know asked how long it would take for me to gather information and meet with him and another man at the Eatonton exit on I-20.

At some point in the conversation, however, he had managed to establish some sort of credibility with me. It may have been the fact that he knew my wife's cousin. For whatever reason, with some mixed emotions, I agreed to the meeting. I kept thinking to myself I had nothing to lose. Besides, it would get me out of the house, and for just a little while, offer a brief respite from the hopelessness that had engulfed me. In my way of thinking, it was probably too late for the miracle that should have happened months ago.

Over the past twenty years, I've had occasions to drive by or even stop and grab a quick bite at this exit. Every time I do, the same movie starts replaying itself in my head. There we were, parked in the Pizza Hut parking lot with rolls of drawings and exhibits sprawled out over the hood of my Rodeo truck. Without going into any great detail, I flatly stated the amount of equity that was in the project and the circumstances that had put us into this precarious situation. I'm sure I made it clear that time was of the essence and expressed my doubts about having enough time to make a deal. Nevertheless, I could sense that these guys seemed anxious to grab the plans and run. All they told me was they had a friend in Atlanta who was always looking for a deal. They also emphasized that if they were successful, my wife's cousin would be compensated, which I assumed would be the case, since they claimed to be business associates.

With my plans and exhibits tucked under their arms, they took off for Atlanta. With only days left before the bank started proceedings, I didn't give these guys a snowball's chance of making something happen. It was late in the day on a Friday, but it was much too late in the game.

Early the following Monday, I received a call from a gentleman by the name of Jim Shelton. He asked if John and I could drive over to Atlanta to meet with him and some of his associates. I was still skeptical and questioned his motives for wanting more information. My thought, based on previous experience, was that he was fishing. He just wanted us to provide the bait which would give him the inside track when buying the project out of foreclosure.

I agreed to the meeting, rounded up John and the two of us made a bee-line to Atlanta. As expected, it followed the script of many of our past meetings. We made our spiel and they probed us for minute details, even as to where the garbage was buried on site.

I noticed a marked difference between this meeting and previous meetings: the people in attendance included a couple of guys from Hilton Head who had developed a course on the island and clearly had experience in golf course operations. I began thinking to myself that surely these guys could see the property's potential for creating some great golf holes. It was obvious they had the experience and credentials to complete the project, and they asked all the right questions. In spite of these hopeful signs, we knew that the difficulty would hinge on money.

In all our other meetings, getting someone to assume Nakamura's 74% equity position had consistently been the deal-breaker. Now we were out of options; we had no leverage, no other takers—we were out of time, and our last resort was to somehow sell the project outright.

As with all our other potential investors, we provided the numbers supporting the amount of outstanding debt and the millions Nakamura had contributed to date. It was a big number, and though this group didn't react in any obvious way, John and I chalked it up to another lost cause as we headed back home.

On a Tuesday the following week Zack called with what I was sure would be more details about the endless legalities we were facing. I remember verbatim his words, "Who are these guys in Atlanta?" I responded, "Some guys we made a presentation to last week." His next remark thundered in my ear, almost knocking me off my feet: "I think these guys are going to do the deal. They've instructed me to set up a closing for this Friday."

Could this actually be happening? A resounding, warm assurance embraced me, and at that moment I knew God had answered our prayers. The roller coaster we had been riding the last two years was about to come to a screeching halt. I was thrilled beyond belief with the news, but strangely. letting go of a dream that had consumed me for the last eight years felt like a death in the family—a devastating loss, one that would be hard to heal.

Friday came and the scheduled closing took place at 4:00 that afternoon. The attorney representing the buyer sat at one end of the table and John and I sat at the other end, with Zack sat in the middle. Before starting, the attorney made a declaration setting the tone for the entire closing. "There will be no other negotiations, no mention of future involvement as designers, partners, or advisors. All work product—drawings, permits and exhibits—will become the property of my client." He continued by saying. "I've been instructed to stop the closing, pack up and return to Atlanta if these terms are violated." That's a great way to start a meeting, wouldn't you say? But that's a lawyer being a lawyer. All I wanted to do was sign some papers and get the hell out. All I wanted from Zack was the assurance that the bank note was settled and vendors paid in full.

My preference would have been for the City of North Augusta or one of the local investor groups to purchase the property and pick up the equity, but it just didn't work out that way.

A vision is not about seeing things as they are, but seeing what they can become. For Henry Schultz, it was a town which he named Hamburg; for Mr. Knox it was an amusement park. My vision was to restore a part of God's creation to its original beauty by getting rid of an unsightly garbage dump and rebuilding the wetlands around it in order to create some great golf holes on the banks of the Savannah River. My vision had taken me captive, consumed me, chewed me up, and left me drained and broken, both financially and in spirit.

Where could I go from there and find the courage to move on? I knew I wasn't alone. I had claimed God's promise that He would never leave me or forsake me. As distasteful as it was to let go of my vision and sell the project—to let it go and have someone else chase "my" great dream—through it all, God had answered my prayers and performed a miracle. The miracle was that John and I could walk away from that closing with our shirts on.

I recently read an article entitled, "Think Like a Champion," by Jim Fannin, a noted mental game coach. He has a 5-second rule where he says, "To think like a champion, you've got to have a short memory. Whether you hit a good shot or a bad shot, you can only think about it for five seconds — then re-boot your brain and focus your thoughts on hitting the shot out in front of you."

In Philippians 3:13, the apostle Paul has a similar rule: "One thing I do, forgetting those things which are behind and reaching forward for those things which are ahead..." I learned that verse as a kid, and now it was time to apply it to my life.

"Forget what is behind" is easy to say but extremely difficult to do. Now I had to re-boot my brain and focus on reclaiming my marriage. It wasn't accepting the loss of a vision that has been the greatest challenge of my life — it has been picking up the pieces of a broken marriage and putting my family back together. This has taken a lot of work, a lot of time, and a lot of healing. I take no credit for it. It has only been God's Grace and the prayers of faithful friends and family that have sustained us.

Years ago I had another vision: I call it my 'original vision,' the one I have steadfastly refused to let go of. It was the dream of a teenager growing up on the south side of Augusta in a place called Nellieville, whose future looked pretty bleak. His vision wasn't extraordinary: in it, he saw himself one day meeting the love of his life, marrying her, and having a family. He knew what he wanted, but at that time and place, it seemed unattainable.

God is good, and in 1970, at the insistence of a friend and co-worker, I met Brenda, my future bride. She turned out to be the girl I thought I'd never find, the one in my vision. After we were married, she's the one who encouraged me to

At long last, the transformation of North Augusta's riverfront has been realized, in this view of the River Golf Club, a beautiful public course.

finish college; the one who worked tirelessly to make sure I graduated; the only one who never complained as we moved from place to place and job to job. Most importantly, she's the one who gave me two fine sons and threw newspapers at 4:00 every morning so she could be a stay-at-home mom and watch them grow up. I could enumerate all her outstanding qualities, including her good looks and her intelligence, but I won't. I don't want her to lose her humility, if you know what I mean!

The reality of my dreams? It's so much more than a kid from Nellieville could have ever imagined. Thanks be to God we are still living the truly important and meaningful part of that vision.

Keep dreaming... keep swinging... keep it in the short grass.

PHOTO: ASHLEY BENNETT

The River Golf Club's 16th green.

"Finally, brothers,
whatever is true, whatever
is noble, whatever is right,
whatever is pure, whatever is
lovely, whatever is admirable
— if anything is excellent or
praiseworthy — think about
such things."

PHILLIPPIANS 4:8

ABOUT THE AUTHOR

Marshall H. "Mark" Bennett, an Augusta native, is a lifelong golfer and course designer who originally planned a career as a commercial artist, seeking a degree in Fine Arts. His schooling was interrupted by a four-year stint in the military working as a commercial artist and medical illustrator during the Vietnam War era.

Upon his discharge, Mr. Bennett was employed by a golf course builder where he became interested in golf course architecture. He returned to school at the University of Georgia, earning a Bachelor of Arts degree in Landscape Architecture with a major emphasis on golf course architecture.

Mr. Bennett served as an apprentice to the notable golf course architect, George Cobb, who designed such noted courses as Quail Hollow Country Club and Carmel Country Club in Charlotte, NC and the famed Par Three Course at the Augusta National Golf Club. Mr. Bennett was exposed to Mr. Cobb's philosophy that great golf courses are those that people enjoy playing and how to properly utilize the natural elements.

Desiring to gain additional experience in related planning, Mr. Bennett took a position with Taft Bradshaw and Associates, Landscape Architects and Planners in Fort Lauderdale, Florida as a Land Planner and worked on such noted projects as Doral Country Club and Bonaventure.

Upon his return home to Augusta, Georgia in 1977 to start his family, Mr. Bennett, now a registered Landscape Architect, founded B/T Design Group, Landscape Architects, Golf Course Architects and Land Planners. B/T Design concentrated their efforts in master planning golf course communities, subdivision and multi-family projects.

Augusta Golf Course Designs, founded in 1991 by Mr. Bennett, specializes in golf course design and is dedicated to promoting the game of golf by designing challenging, but enjoyable, golf courses. His concept is to create a golf course which will be just as enticing to a member ten years hence as it is today whether he be a professional or a 36-handicapper. Mr. Bennett's experience includes working with notable professional golfers Ken Venturi and Raymond Floyd.

Mr. Bennett designs courses that are natural, that relate very carefully to the land and do not require a tremendous amount of earth moving, always keeping in mind the strategy of the game and the elements that provide beauty in the golf courses. He fully ascribes to the design philosophy of Robert Trent Jones: "A golf course should provide considerable natural beauty, enjoyable for the average golfer, and at the same time, testing the expert player striving to better par. We want to make the bogeys easy, if frankly sought, pars readily obtainable by good standard play, and birdies, except on par fives, dearly bought."

ACKNOWLEDGEMENTS

This book would not exist without the encouragement and prayers of many friends and family members who believe this is a story that needs telling. The takeaway for all who read it is "Quitting is not an option."

To those who have given of their time and talent in editing and offering suggestions for a compelling read, I offer many thanks.

In my quest as to where to start the publishing process, I want to thank Roger Enevoldsen, a long time friend who took the time to read my first draft and offer suggestions for improvement. A special thanks to Yvonne Sobel for her many hours of word-smithing in proofing my Southern grammar and her relentless encouragement in completing the work. Boundless love and gratitude go to my two boys, Jason and Ashley, who have pushed me to share my story with others.

A special thanks to Don Bagwell, a long-time friend and graphic designer from my college days who tirelessly persevered to edit and organize my story in its present form and whose skill created the book's layout and cover design. I am extremely blessed to be surrounded by such generous and talented friends.

Finally, thanks to my beautiful wife Brenda, who dared to be a dreamer with me—who doesn't look back but continues to be the girl I married, a person of unusual inner strength and beauty. Her many talents, outside of being a wife, mother, grandmother and caregiver, include her mastery of the English language, her typing skills, and her ability to lovingly serve as my number one critic: that's the quality I most appreciate. I'm forever thankful for her love, knowing I've been blessed.

Grateful acknowledgement is made to the following sources as background for historical accounts and references in this book:

James C. and Lucien E. Roberts, Eds. Bonner. *Studies in Georgia History and Government* (UGA Press, Athens, GA, 1940)

Edward J. Cashin. *The Story of Augusta*. Reprint Co., 1991.

North Augusta Historical Society. *The History of North Augusta, SC*, published 1980.

NOTES

The conceptual rendering of Henry Schultz on page 17 was illustrated by Don M. Bagwell.

The engraving of the Augusta Bridge 1816 on page 21 is taken from Henry Schultz' Bridge Bank currency, provided courtesy of Carl A. Anderson and David Marsh, *Georgia Obsolete Currency*.

The 1891 aerial map of Hamburg, SC on page 22 was drafted by Albert Langley.

The Bird's Eye View of Augusta 1872 on page 23 was illustrated by C. N. Drie.

CPSIA information can be obtained
at www.ICGtesting.com
Printed in the USA
FFOW04n1545060416
23014FF